Revelations of God's Love:
Your Treasure Map to His Heart

By

His utility handmaiden,

Gail P. Miller

Published by
Queen V Publishing
Englewood, OH
QueenVPublishing.com

Published by
Queen V Publishing
Englewood, OH
QueenVPublishing.com

Copyright © 2023 by Gail P. Miller

All rights reserved. No part of this book can be reproduced in any form without written permission from the author. The author guarantees all writings are original works and do not infringe upon the legal rights of any other person living or deceased.

Unless otherwise noted, Scripture references are taken from The Holy Bible, New King James Version Copyright © 1982 by Thomas Nelson, Inc. Used by permission. All rights reserved.

Library of Congress Catalog Number: 2023915616

ISBN-13: 978-0-9794489-3-5

Edited by Valerie J. Lewis Coleman of Pen of the Writer

Proofread by Sharahnne Gibbons of Something in Comma

Author photo by Glamour Shots

Printed in the United States of America

Praise for Revelations of God's Love

"Gail P. Miller went deep into the Word to uncover how to love yourself through the lens of God."
—Elder Charles R. Byrd, Ph.D., pastor of Apostolic House of Christ

"*Revelations of God's Love* is holy, coming directly from the heart of God. I encourage you to read this book to experience the beauty, power, and mystery of God's passionate love for you. You will not be disappointed."
—Dr. Diane M. Parks-Love, pastor of Liberated In Christ Ministries, Inc.

"Do you want to draw closer to God? Read this book and ask the Holy Spirit to alter your heart and renew your mind. Gail P. Miller unlocked divine teachings that will leave imprints on your heart."
—Elder Marcia T. Raglin, Ethan Temple Seven-Day Adventist Church

"Seasoned Christians, new converts, and scholars can use *Revelations of God's Love* to develop an intimate relationship with Him. This book is an excellent resource for group study or persons who desire an introspective walk with Christ."
—Connie Y. Beal, teacher and educator

"In this exposition, you will experience the Almighty's thoughts and ways that can only be explained by a vessel who invested time in His presence. As you search this treasure map of God's heart, His power and passion will emanate from the pages."
—Minister JL Dubose, member of Faith Chapel Christian Center

"*Revelations of God's Love* had me turning pages late into the night. Gail P. Miller's book helps you find a sense of purpose when life seems meaningless. If something deep inside you longs for answers, this book will help your spiritual journey."

—Graciela R. McLaughlin, president of Amazing Grace Empowerment Ministries, Inc.

Dedication

Revelations of God's Love is dedicated to my son, Darrell N. Miller, grandsons, Darrell (Antanae) Miller II, Jarrell Miller, great grandson, Darrell Miller III, my grandsons' mother, Alishia Wood, and Grandma Sherri Taylor who is like a sister to me.

Antanae's family: her mother, Crystal Eke, sister, Breanna Eke, and brother, Christian McCain.

And to the loving memories of family, friends, and saints who are now with the Lord.

His Utility Handmaiden

God named me His utility handmaiden when I was in a place of brokenness. Like a wall outlet that does not control the power coming through it, I am there to release His power. Like a faucet that cannot turn on by itself, I give water for cleansing or quenching. Like a phone receiver waiting for someone to accept the call, I serve as a conduit to deliver the message.

God revealed that people have utility closets filled with a variety of tools. He chose me to be His cornucopia because I am His hand tool ready to be used for His purpose and endowed with the fruit of His Spirit.

Revelations of God's Love

Table of Contents

Foreword 13
Introduction 15
Lessons of Love 17
Lesson 1 A Two-Way Street 19
    Lesson 1 Questions 23
    Lesson 1 Answers 25
Lesson 2 Forgive is a Compound Word 27
    Lesson 2 Questions 31
    Lesson 2 Answers 35
Lesson 3 Love Never Fails 37
    Lesson 3 Questions 43
    Lesson 3 Answers 47
Lesson 4 Heaven's Currency 49
    Lesson 4 Questions 53
    Lesson 4 Answers 55
Lesson 5 The Love of Money 57
    Lesson 5 Questions 63
    Lesson 5 Answers 65

Lesson 6 Love Chastens 67
   Lesson 6 Questions 71
   Lesson 6 Answers 73
Lesson 7 No Boundaries 75
   Lesson 7 Questions 79
   Lesson 7 Answers 81
Lesson 8 Love Defeated the Real Bully 83
   Lesson 8 Questions 95
   Lesson 8 Answers 97
Lesson 9 Your Example 99
   Lesson 9 Questions 105
   Lesson 9 Answers 107
Lesson 10 Living By Every Word 109
   Lesson 10 Questions 117
   Lesson 10 Answers 119
Love Notes 121
   Love's Mercy 123
   Love Transformed Himself for You 125
   Love's Comparisons 127
   Love's Questionnaire 129
   Love's Health Plan 131
   Love Draws with Loving Kindness 134
   Love Teaches 136
   Love Can Be Followed 139

The Fragrance of Love 141
Love is a Weapon 143
Chords of Love 145
　Do You Need a Hug? 147
　Love's Grace Is Sufficient! 149
　Love Wants to Know! 151
　Love Was There! 152
　Love's Trade Off! 154
　Let Love Answer! 155
　Love Already Died! 157
　It's Love's Word! 159
　There's No Competition! 161
　Love Saves! 163
Dewdrops of Love 165
　Hard Times! 167
　You Were Still Planned! 169
　Every Day! 171
　You Are Unique! 173
　Take A Look! 174
　Do You Have the I-Dust? 176
　From the Beginning of Time! 178
　His Glory was Seen! 180
　Have You Seen Yourself? 182
　No Other Name! 185

It's Not Just! 186

We Still Have! 188

Acknowledgements 191

About the Author 193

About Queen V Publishing 195

Revelations of God's Love

Foreword

If any of you lacks wisdom, he should ask God who gives generously to all without finding fault, and it will be given to him.
—James 1:5 NIV[1]

Wisdom can be used as a tool to learn how things work or to learn from past mistakes. Wisdom is a gift that God gave to mankind to expand our thoughts and experiences with Him and each other. Wisdom will help you if you allow it. When you have a thorough understanding of God's design for your life, you can live to the fullest, being complete and healthy emotionally, mentally, and physically without any fears. Wisdom is essential! It is a building block for your success and wellbeing.

What can I say to persuade you to read this book? Do you want to experience a love that surpasses your current understanding of love? Do you want an indescribable peace? Do you want to understand your life the way God designed it? Do you want to be refreshed or enlightened with answers to questions you have been pondering? Are you curious about the real meaning of life and why you're here?

God has prepared a vessel of honor—whom He designed for this specific purpose—to help you get clarity. She submitted herself to hear and obey the Lord's will. She cried, prayed, and sought the One who is all-knowing to

---

[1] *The Life Application Study Bible*, New International Version, Tyndale House Publisher, Inc. and Zondervan, 2005, p. 2090.

give her the understanding needed to change her life. She knows her life's purpose and is committed to helping you find yours.

If you want to experience this remarkable changing of life, dive into this book. Listen to the poetry of the Lord's voice, it will woo you to Him. Pray and ask God to expand your vision so that you, too, can live victorious in Him!

Rev. Thelma Buchanan

Revelations of God's Love

Introduction

After experiencing several unfaithful failed relationships, I was lonely and broken-hearted. I was the odd one at family events with no one to hold me when I needed it the most. Would anyone notice if I was not there? If I took my own life would anyone care? Feeling sorry for myself, I cried to the Lord, "Why am I rejected?"

Many people experience emotional times about being alone. Wondering if your life has value, if anyone cares, or is this the hand you've been dealt. I now know that it does not have to be like that for you. Why? Because in my despair, I heard Him say, "You have a Love!"

As a Christian, single matriarch, and retired public-school teacher, I have seen, experienced, and created my share of pain, hurt, and loneliness. I discovered that I was not alone and amazingly, rejection is not always a bad thing.

In this study guide, you will work through lessons, questions, examples, and suggested supplemental materials. If you use this book as a teaching tool, students' responses may trigger new questions. Seek the Lord for ideas to make the lessons personal and relevant to your audience.

Throughout the book, you'll find underlined words. I encourage you to research their meanings to enhance understanding. Hebrew definitions for Old Testament text and Greek definitions for New Testament words are underlined for a clearer understanding of the Scriptures.
Revealed in this treasure map are truths that uncover more hidden messages. *Love Notes*, *Chords of Love*, and *Dewdrops of Love* are Scriptures curated to expose His tender mercies,

manifold wisdoms, and love's name as a healing balm to soothe you. They are prophetic poetic psalms of instructions, questions, and prayers to lift you. These revelations are drops of God's encouragement designed to splash light into your heart to foster your praise, prayer, and growth.

Since God is love, love is used interchangeably in reference to God and Jesus.

Everything you ever needed or wanted from love has already been prepared for you. As you embark on this treasure hunt, may you find your heart flowing with love as you search for these cherished deposits of God's heart.

Gail P. Miller

Lessons

of

Love

These were more fair-minded than those in Thessalonica, in that they received the word with all readiness, and searched the Scriptures daily to find out whether these things were so.
— Acts 17:11

Gail P. Miller

Revelations of God's Love

Lesson 1
A Two-Way Street

This lesson illustrates what God says about His love for you. You will uncover what Love set in place for you to love Him. David declared the value of God's Word, what His Word does, and the rewards it gives to those who keep and walk in them.

> *The law if the Lord is perfect, converting the soul; The testimony of the Lord is sure making wise the simple; The statutes of the Lord are right, rejoicing the heart; The commandment of the Lord is pure, enlightening the eyes; The fear of the Lord is clean, enduring forever, the judgments of the Lord are true and righteous all together. More to be desired are they than gold, Yea, than much fine gold; Sweeter also than honey and the honey comb. Moreover by them Your servant is warned, And in keeping them there is great reward.*
> —Psalm 19:7-11

God loves you because His Word, which is true, tells you so and He does not have the ability to lie. Find several Scriptures confirming God's love for you and that He cannot lie. Here is your first clue: Start your search in Numbers and John.

_____

_____

_____

Christ gave His life for you by dying on the cross and pouring out His blood as payment for your sins. Do you love Him? The following verse explains how you are to love God.

> *You shall love the Lord your God with all your heart, with all your soul, and with all your strength.*
> —Deuteronomy 6:5

In addition to Matthew 22:37-39, find Old and New Testament Scriptures that identify the first two commandments of love.

_____

_____

_____

Now that you know the order of love, understand that loving God means keeping His commandments (John 14:15).

Read John 14 to discover how many times Jesus stated how He knows if you love Him. Who did He say is your helper?

_____

_____

_____

Revelations of God's Love

Learning God's Word is important to your relationship with Him and others. Read Acts 17:11 and 2 Timothy 2:15 to understand to whom studying approves you, the kind of mind you have, and the daily search that keeps you in the know.

_____

_____

_____

The following verses give insight about your body, the price paid for it, being born of God, and what hate makes you.

> *"Food for the stomach and the stomach for food, but God will destroy both of them. Now the body is not for sexual immorality but for the Lord, and the Lord for the body. Or do you not know that your body is the temple of the Holy Spirit who is in you, whom you have from God, and you are not your own? For you were bought at a price therefore glorify God in your body and in your spirit, which are God's."*
> —1 Corinthians 6:13, 19-20

Beloved, let us love one another, for love is of God; and everyone who loves is born of God and knows God. He who does not love does not know God, for God is Love. If someone says, 'I love God and hates his brother, he is a liar, for he who does not love his brother whom he has seen, how can he love God whom he has not seen? And this commandment we have from Him: that he who loves God must love his brother also.
—1 John 4:7-8, 20-21

Read Romans 12:1-2 and 1 Corinthians 3:16-17 to understand what will happen if you don't do your part.

_____

_____

_____

Based on the above Scriptures, inventory your life to determine if you line up with His Word.
Do you love God…His way?

Revelations of God's Love

Lesson 1 Questions

1. Will God hold you accountable for studying His Word?
2. How does God know if you do not love Him?
3. If you say that you love God, but don't keep His Word and hate your brother, what are you called?
4. Who will teach you all things and bring to your mind what Jesus said?
5. To whom does your body belong?
6. The question is not does God love you, but do you love God His way?

Suggested materials to make the lesson come alive!
- To study the verses in context, read the entire chapters for Scriptures noted in the lesson. Use a Bible commentary like *Halley's Bible Handbook* or *Liberty Bible Commentary, The Old-Time Gospel Hour Edition*.
- Create a PowerPoint presentation adding your choice of images with each teaching point of the lesson.
- Make posters of Scriptures to hang on the wall, easel, or bulletin board. Make copies for each student.
- Draw pictures of what love means to you.
- Make a poster of a street with opposing lanes of traffic to help visualize love as a two-way street.

Gail P. Miller

Memory Verse

Jesus answered and said to him, "If anyone loves Me, he will keep My Word; and My Father will love him, and We will come to him and make Our home with him."
— John 14:23

Revelations of God's Love

Lesson 1 Answers

The following answers are based on the lesson Scriptures and understanding of the subject matter. Because God's Word is alive, some questions may have answers beyond the ones provided here.

A Two-Way Street!

1. Yes. God holds you accountable for studying—or not studying—His Word. Discuss Acts 17:11 and 2 Timothy 2:15.
2. The person of the age of accountability who does not keep His Word.
3. God calls you a liar, if you claim to love Him, but hate your brother. 1 John 4:8
4. The Holy Spirit will teach you all things and remind you of His Word.
5. Your body belongs to the Lord.
6. You make that determination based on your knowledge of the Word and how you align with it.

Gail P. Miller

Lesson 2
Forgive is a Compound Word

Unforgiveness makes you vulnerable and creates a breach whereas Satan can launch his attacks. Forgiveness can be the doorway out of your bitterness, anger, and wounds whether self-inflected or by others. These hurts can be destroyed by God's loving kindness.

Since forgive is a compound word, let's look at meanings of its parts.

For means:	Give means:
because of	to offer as a gift
on behalf of	to pay as price
in honor of	to hand out, distribute
in support of	to yield to give in
in favor of	to cause to have
with the purpose of	to grant, confer
for the benefit of	to allow, permit
destined to	to render as being due
in spite of	to deliver a message
for all that, "nevertheless"	to bestow charity[2]

Using the above definitions, develop your own meanings for a better understanding of forgive. You can see

---

[2] *The New Lexicon Webster's Dictionary of the English Language,* Encyclopedic Edition, Lexicon Publications, Inc. New York. 1989 Edition.

what Jesus did for you and in return, what you have to do for yourself and others.

1. _____
2. _____
3. _____
4. _____
5. _____
6. _____
7. _____

> *But if you do not forgive men their trespasses, neither will your Father forgive your trespasses.*
> — Matthew 6:15[3]

In the above Scripture, Greek meanings for forgive (863, Greek af-ee'-ay-nee) include to send, forsake, lay aside, omit, suffer, separation, and reverse. Further study reveals more explanation.

(575, Greek apó) off, away, as a prefix, separation, departure, reversal, cessation, disembark

(5375, Hebrew naw-saw') to lift, accept, cast, receive, yield, help

(5545, Hebrew saw-lakh) forgive, pardon, spare [4]

---

[3] *The Holy Bible*, New King James Version, by Thomas Nelson Inc. 1982.
[4] *The New Strong's Exhaustive Concordance of the Bible,* James Strong's LL.D., S.T.D. Nashville, Thomas Nelson Publishers TN, 1990.

Read Matthew 18:21-35. How many times are you to forgive someone? What comparison is made about the kingdom? What will God do to you if you don't forgive?

_____

_____

_____

Read Micha 7:19. What does God do with sin when you seek His forgiveness?

_____

_____

_____

But if you do not forgive, neither will your Father in heaven forgive your trespasses.
—Mark 11:26

Read Mark 11:23-26. What happens to your prayers when you operate in unforgiveness?

_____

_____

_____

To offer forgiveness to someone who has hurt or offended you, first pray for them. Ask God to forgive them and help you move past the situation without bitterness, anger, or unloving residue. Depending upon the circumstance and your desire to restore the relationship, you can speak to them to express your feelings. If you choose to meet in person, consider taking someone with you. Another option is to write a letter. Whether you give them the letter, burn it, or keep it for yourself, is up to you. The process of pouring your heart onto the pages can be therapeutic.

In broken relationships where the other person died, is not willing to forgive, or has forgiven you but does not desire a relationship, know that everything will be okay as long as you have forgiven the offender and the offence. Your healing may take a while, but you are free in Him.

God is your healer. Go to Him for help!

Revelations of God's Love

Lesson 2 Questions

1. What does God do to you when you do not forgive others?
2. Should you forgive yourself?
3. Can your past or present pains, hurts, or experiences, keep you from forgiving others?
4. From where do you have to forgive people?
5. Will God excuse you from forgiving others because of what has happened to you?
6. What does forgiveness do to a relationship?

Forgiveness[5]

Matters left unresolved can grow like a deep-rooted weed causing resentfulness, bitterness, and physical ailments.

Forgiveness transforms anger and hurt into healing and peace. Forgiveness can help you overcome depression, anxiety, and rage. Forgiveness gives you the power to resolve personal and relational conflicts. When you make a conscious decision to release a grudge, hurt, or disappointment, you take control, stand in your power, and own your worth. Forgiveness is not for the other person, but yourself.

Note: You do not have to confront or speak directly to the offender to offer forgiveness. It's an inside job between you and God.

This activity will help you identify, forgive, and release past hurts.

---

[5] *Pen of the Writer Mentoring: Forgiveness,* Valerie J. Lewis Coleman. PenOfTheWriter.com.

1. List things for which you have not forgiven others.

   _____
   _____
   _____

2. List things for which you have not forgiven yourself.

   _____
   _____
   _____

3. Thank God for forgiving you for offenses you committed knowingly and unknowingly. Ask Him to forgive you for holding onto unforgiveness. Accept that every mistake has within it an opportunity for you to grow, mature and improve.

   _____
   _____
   _____

4. For each offender and offense, say,

    "Lord, I choose to forgive _____ from my heart for _____. Lord, is there anything else I need to forgive _____ for? I declare _____ is no longer in my debt. _____ is no longer taking up energy and space in my life. Father, bless _____. I release _____ to Your highest good."

    _____

    _____

    _____

5. Recite the following prayer daily:

    Father, I ask that You create in me a clean heart and renew a right spirit within me. I send forgiveness ahead of me to release anyone who sins against me in word, deed, or action. I will not take on another man's offence. I will ask for forgiveness when I realize that I have hurt someone and You. In Jesus' name, amen.

    Psalm 51:10; Mark 11:26; 1 John 1:9, Micah 7:19.

If the offender is deceased, write a letter expressing what they did and how it affected you. If possible, read it at their gravesite or speak your heart. Once forgiveness has been given, destroy the letter. Watching it burn has metaphysical benefits to you as the ashes float away. Be sure to thank God for mending your heart.

Suggested materials to make the lesson come alive!
- To study the verses in context, read the entire chapters for Scriptures noted in the lesson. Use a Bible commentary like *Halley's Bible Handbook* or *Liberty Bible Commentary, The Old-Time Gospel Hour Edition*.
- Create original quotes or search the internet for quotes that deal with unforgiveness. Make posters, a PowerPoint presentation, and/or copies of the collected quotes to share.
- Read *Will You Forgive Me?* by Sally Grindley and Penny Dann to younger children.
- Explore *"and he has nothing in Me"* in John 14:30 as it relates to unforgiveness. Hebrews 4:15 and 9:28 provide further understanding of this phrase.

Memory Verse

But if you do not forgive men their trespasses, neither will your Father forgive your trespasses.
—Matthew 6:15

Lesson 2 Answers

The following answers are based on the lesson Scriptures and understanding of the subject matter. Because God's Word is alive, some questions may have answers beyond the ones provided here.

Forgive is a Compound Word!

1. God will not forgive you and He will deliver you to the torturers. Matthew 6:15, 18:23-35
2. Yes. John 3:17; 1 John 1:9
3. Yes, if you let them. These things can be the reasons for not forgiving others. Seek help in the form of prayer and speaking with your pastor, a counselor, professional therapist, or psychologist. Support groups can also provide assistance.
4. From you heart. Matthew 18:35
5. No. Matthew 6:15, 18:35; Mark 11:25
6. Forgiveness can heal, restore, and reunite broken relationships.

Binding and loosing also apply to forgiveness and unforgiveness. Matthew 18:15-18, 23-35. Per Romans 13:8, you owe it to all mankind to love and forgive.

Gail P. Miller

Revelations of God's Love

Lesson 3
Love Never Fails

Titles—bishop, evangelist, prophet—casting out demons, giving to the poor, or having great faith does not mean that heaven is your final destination.

> *Not everyone who says to Me, Lord, Lord, shall enter the kingdom of heaven, but he who does the will of My Father in heaven. Many will say to Me in that day, Lord, Lord, have we not prophesied in Your name, cast out demons in Your name, and done many wonders in Your name? And then I will declare to them, I never knew you; depart from Me, you who practice lawlessness!*
> —Matthew 7:21-23

Read 1 Corinthians 13:1-3 to see what these actions yield when done without love. Compare this passage to Matthew 7:21-23.

_____

_____

_____

In 1 Corinthians 13:3, the Greek definition of profiteth/profits (Gk. o-fel-eh'-o) means to be useful, to benefit, advantage, prevail, or profit.[6]

Read these Scriptures for more understanding:
- Proverbs 10:12, 17:9, 17
- Matthew 5:43-48
- 1 John 4:8, 20-21

_____

_____

_____

The Greek meaning of God's unconditional love (ag-ah'-pay) means love, affection or benevolence, a love feast.[7]

For further clarification, read 1 Corinthians 13:4-8a. With the following Scripture, discuss how love behaves.

> *Now concerning things offered to idols: we know that we all have knowledge. Knowledge puffs up, but love edifies.*
> – 1 Corinthians 8:1

In the above verse, edifies (3618, Greek oy-kod-om-eh'-o) means to be a housebuilder, construct or confirm (be in) build (-er, -ing, up), edify, embolden.[8]

---

[6] *The New Strong's Exhaustive Concordance of the Bible,* James Strong's LL.D., S.T.D. Nashville, TN, by Thomas Nelson Publishers, 1990.
[7] Ibid.
[8] *The New Strong's Exhaustive Concordance of the Bible,* James Strong's LL.D., S.T.D. Nashville, TN, by Thomas Nelson Publishers, 1990.

These Scriptures reveal how you are to act when you walk in God's kind of love. Read John 3:16 with gave defined within the bracketed text.

> *For God so loved the world that He <u>gave</u>* [ministered, committed, suffered, offered, delivered, or yielded up][9] *His only begotten Son, that whoever believes in Him shall not perish but have eternal life.*
> —John 3:16

Re-read John 3:16 replacing gave with each word in the brackets.

> *Love never fails. But whether there are prophecies, they will fail; whether there are tongues, they will cease; whether there is knowledge, it will vanish away.*
> —1 Corinthians 13:8

In this passage, "never fails" means the following:
- never drops away
- never is driven off of one's course
- never becomes inefficient
- never loses its effect
- never is out of place, time, or cause
- never falls down or off[10]

The opposite means that prophecies, tongues, and knowledge will eventually stop and become useless.

---

[9] Ibid.
[10] Ibid.

Everything you do in word or deed; God says that you are to do it in love. Spiritually, love gives life to these things. Read Colossians 3:12-14, James 2:1-8, and 1 John 3:15-18 for further understanding.

Love defined…

> *Beloved, let us love one another, for love is of God; and everyone who loves is born of God and knows God. He who does not love does not know God, for God is Love.*
> —1 John 4:7-8

Read 1 Corinthians 13:1-9. Note and/or discuss what you observed.

_____

_____

_____

You only know and speak prophecies, tongues, and knowledge as the Holy Spirit reveals them to you. Therefore, as you mature in the fullness of Christ, the hidden things in God's Word (Bible) will be unveiled. His purpose for you will come forth when you continually obey His Word. The Genesis 1:26 image and likeness will be formed in you, and only then can you see His face in peace.

> *Let us make man in our image, according to our likeness.*
> —Genesis 1: 26

We shall be like Him.
—1 John 3:2b

The following is a definition of God's agapé love given by the Holy Spirit through Dr. Diane M. Parks-Love, in my book, *True Love Has a Passion for You!*

> "Agapé is the love that asks only to be accepted. Agapé is the love that God gives in spite of who we are or are not. Agapé is the love that offers to transform us into the vessels that we were born to be according to God's purpose. Agapé is the love that defines Truth: "For God so loved the world that He gave..." Agapé is the love that gave Christ Jesus to the world. Agapé is the love that gives man the opportunity to have eternal life through Christ. Agapé is the love that is supernatural and indefinable. Agape' is true passion."[11]

Love is known by its fruits!

---

[11] Miller, Gail P., *True Love Has a Passion for You!* Queen V Publishing, Englewood, OH.

Gail P. Miller

Revelations of God's Love

Lesson 3 Questions

1. Can your gifts and calling work without love?
2. What kind of sounds are you making when you act without love?
3. What is the opposite of profits or profiteth?
4. With whom is there no profit or benefit when a person ministers without God's love: God or mankind?
5. How does the God kind of love act?
6. What is the main thing love does?
7. Since God is love, then love is a what?
8. Which is the greatest of faith, hope, and love?
9. Why is it the greatest of the three?
10. What does "knew" mean in Matthew 7:23?

Suggested materials to make the lesson come alive!
- To study the verses in context, read the entire chapters for Scriptures noted in the lesson. Use a Bible commentary like *Halley's Bible Handbook* or *Liberty Bible Commentary, The Old-Time Gospel Hour Edition*.
- Read Matthew 7:15-20; Luke 9:23; James 1:21-25.
- Create a PowerPoint presentation adding your choice of images with each teaching point of the lesson.
- Make posters of Scriptures to hang on the wall, easel, or bulletin board. Make copies for each student.
- Draw pictures of what love means to you.
- Use a large container, a small container, and water to illustrate how a person can be near the

Word, talk about the Word, sing about the Word, repeat the Word, but not obey the Word.

<u>Example 1</u>
1. Get a clear tub, pitcher, or bucket. Fill it half-way with water.
2. Get a cup, water bottle, or small container with a water-tight top.
3. Place the small container beside the larger one.
4. The water in the larger vessel represents God and His Word. The smaller container represents a person or believer.
5. Understand that a person can be near God's Word, hear God's Word, speak God's Word, see God's Word in action, go to church, and be around people who know God's Word, but if they have not been born again, it is useless. Hold up the empty vessel. Explain that salvation is not transferable. You cannot be saved because your grandmother, friend or other family members are saved. Joining a church and being active in ministry does not save you. Only when you invite Jesus into your heart can you experience salvation for yourself.

<u>Example 2</u>
1. Repeat steps 1 and 2 in Example 1.
2. Place the small container with the top firmly closed in the large container.
3. Explain that a believer can do good works—singing, teaching, serving in the ministry—but if they do not live by God's Word, they are deceived. 1 Samuel 15:22; James 1:22-25.

Example 3
1. Repeat steps 1 and 2 in Example 1.
2. Remove the lid from the small container.
3. Place the small container in the larger one.
4. Explain that once you make the choice to accept Christ as your personal Savior, you must be open to receive and live by God's Word.

Memory Verse

Love never fails. But whether there are prophecies, they will fail; whether there are tongues, they will cease; whether there is knowledge, it will vanish away.
—1 Corinthians 13:8

Gail P. Miller

Revelations of God's Love

Lesson 3 Answers

The following answers are based on the lesson Scriptures and understanding of the subject matter. Because God's Word is alive, some questions may have answers beyond the ones provided here.

Love Never Fails!

1. Yes.
2. A sounding brass or a clanging cymbal. 1 Corinthians 13:1
3. Not useful, no benefit, no advantage, not prevailing, or no profit.
4. God!
5. 1 Corinthians 13:4-7 and word definitions.
6. Give.
7. Who.
8. Love. 1 Corinthians 13:13
9. Because God is love, (1 John 4:8), and He created all things (Colossians 1:16-19), therefore, faith and hope operate by love. 1 Corinthians 13:13; 1 Peter 1:21
10. Knew (1097, Greek ghin-oce'-ko) to 'know' allow, be aware (of), feel (have) know (-ledge), perceive, be resolved, can speak, be sure, understand.[12]

---

[12] *The New Strong's Exhaustive Concordance of the Bible,* James Strong's LL.D., S.T.D. Nashville, TN, by Thomas Nelson Publishers, 1990.

Gail P. Miller

Lesson 4
Heaven's Currency

Currency is defined as coins, notes, or other tokens in circulation as a means of <u>exchange</u> (paper bank notes, cash, bills, legal tender, coinage, or a piece of metal money). All of which are recognized by a country's authority, government, or in this case, kingdom.[13]

What do you use currency to buy?

_____

_____

_____

God's Kingdom has a different currency or means of exchange.

> *Ho! Everyone who thirst, come to the waters; and you who have no <u>money</u>, come, buy, and eat. Yes, come, buy wine and milk without <u>money</u> and without price.*
> —Isaiah 55:1

---

[13] *The New Lexicon Webster's Dictionary of The English Language,* Encyclopedic Edition, Lexicon Publications, Inc. New York. 1989 Edition.

In this passage, money (3701, Hebrew keh'-sef) means silver, money, price, silver (-ling).[14] What price will you give in exchange for the food and drink God mentioned in Isaiah 55:1?

_____

_____

_____

> *For God so loved the world that He gave His only begotten <u>Son</u>, that whoever believes in Him should not perish but have everlasting life.*
> —John 3:16

In this Scripture, son (5207, Greek hwee-os') means a son, kinship: child, foal, son.[15] Choose one of the meanings of son to fill in the blank and re-read for more understanding.

> *For God so loved the world that He gave His only begotten _____, that whoever believes in [His] _____ should not perish but have everlasting life.*
> —John 3:16 rephrased with love as noted

What type of word is "so"? Look up its Greek meaning.

_____

_____

_____

---

[14]*The New Strong's Exhaustive Concordance of the Bible,* James Strong's LL.D., S.T.D. Nashville, TN, by Thomas Nelson Publishers, 1990.
[15] Ibid.

Revelations of God's Love

Substitute the definitions for "so" in the blank and read it again.

> *For God _____ loved the world that He gave his only begotten Son, that whosoever believes in Him should not perish but have everlasting life.*
> —John 3:16

With this new understanding and the definition of currency, which of the following words best gives you knowledge of the legal tender of heaven? **The Word, The Lamb, or Love.**

> _____, is a system of money (legal tender, cash bills, notes, coins, banknotes, or coinage) in general use in a particular country or in the kingdom of heaven. The coin, note, or other token in circulation as a means of <u>exchange</u> is _____ in God's House.

Read Isaiah 55:1-11 to understand what happens when heaven's currency is given in exchange for your sins.

_____

_____

_____

What price was paid for you to have everlasting life?

Have you received and accepted your heavenly currency?

Gail P. Miller

Revelations of God's Love

Lesson 4 Questions

1. What is in circulation as a means of exchange for your salvation?
2. How much does everlasting life cost?
3. How did God express His love for you?
4. What Scriptures confirm it?
5. Do the invitations in Isaiah 55:1 and John 3:16 include you?
6. What is God offering those invited in Isaiah 55:1-9 and John 3:16-17?
7. Are God's thoughts and ways the same as yours?
8. Do you have to let go of your thoughts and ways to turn to the Lord?

Suggested materials to make the lesson come alive!
- To study the verses in context, read the entire chapters for Scriptures noted in the lesson. Use a Bible commentary like *Halley's Bible Handbook* or *Liberty Bible Commentary, The Old-Time Gospel Hour Edition*.
- Create a PowerPoint presentation adding your choice of images with each teaching point of the lesson. For example, money, a cross, books, bible, empty box, the sky, or heaven.
- Make a poster of money and Jesus or love to compare the currencies.
- Make posters of Scriptures to hang on the wall, easel, or bulletin board. Make copies for each student.
- Draw pictures of what love means to you.

Gail P. Miller

Memory Verse

For God so loved the world that He gave His only begotten Son, that whoever believes in Him should not perish but have everlasting life.
—John 3:16

Revelations of God's Love

Lesson 4 Answers

The following answers are based on the lesson Scriptures and understanding of the subject matter. Because God's Word is alive, some questions may have answers beyond the ones provided here.

Heavens Currency!

1. Jesus. He gave His life.
2. Other than your obedience to Him, everlasting life is free.
3. Through Jesus Christ, His death on the cross, His shed blood for the atonement of your sin, His burial, and His resurrection.
4. Romans 5:8 and others.
5. Yes.
6. A renewed relationship with God, forgiveness of sins, salvation, and everlasting life.
7. No.
8. Yes. Isaiah 55:7

Note: The fill-in-the-blank activity on page 51 lists names by which Jesus is called as He relates to currency.

Gail P. Miller

Lesson 5
The Love of Money

A man with an <u>evil</u> eye hastens after riches, and does not consider that poverty will come upon Him.
—Proverbs 28:22

For the <u>love</u> of <u>money</u> is a <u>root</u> of all kinds of <u>evil</u>, for which some have strayed from the faith in their greediness, and pierced themselves through with many sorrows.
—1 Timothy 6:10

The following Greek definitions give a clearer understanding of how this kind of love holds one to evil.
- <u>Evil</u> (2556, Greek kak-os'): worthless, depraved, or injurious: bad, evil, harm, ill, noisome, wicked
- <u>Love</u> (5365, Greek fil-ar-goo-ree'ah): avarice (extreme, insatiable greed) fond of silver, covetous, friendly, an associate, neighbor, (shinning) silver (the metal, in the articles or coin)
- <u>Money</u> (5365, Greek fil-ar-goo-ree'ah): avarice (extreme, insatiable greed) love of money (same as love definition)
- <u>Root</u> (4491, Greek hrid'-zah): root. Dictionary:[16] that part of the plant which in most species penetrates the

---

[16] *The New Lexicon Webster's Dictionary of the English Language Encyclopedia Edition*, Lexicon Publication, Inc. New York, 1989 Edition.

earth, absorbs moisture, stores food, and also serves as an anchor and support[17]

Did you notice that love and money have the same meaning in this verse? This kind of love fosters greed and other kinds of evil.

Read, discuss, or think about Matthew 6:19-21, Mark 4:18-19, and 1 John 2:15-17.

_____

_____

_____

From these Scriptures, you can glean the following understandings:
- Your heart is tied to the treasure that you love whether earthly or heavenly.
- The Word sown in your heart can be choked out by the cares of this world or deceitful riches including money.
- Wrong desires can make the Word in you unfruitful or barren.
- Loving the world and the things in it reveals the kind of love in you.

No one can serve two masters, for either he will hate the one and love the other, or else he will be loyal to the one and despise the other. You cannot serve God and <u>mammon</u>.
—Matthew 6:24

---

[17] *The New Strong's Exhaustive Concordance of the Bible,* James Strong's LL.D., S.T.D. Nashville, TN, by Thomas Nelson Publishers, 1990.

The Greek meaning of mammon (man-mo-nae') is confidence, wealth, avarice (extreme, insatiable greed, deified).[18]

God and mammon are masters, which makes one a slave to the master chosen to serve. Read, discuss, or think about the following Scriptures to understand what some people believe about godliness.

> *Do you not know that to whom you present yourselves slaved to obey, you are that one's slaves whom you obey, whether of sin leading to death, or of obedience leading to righteousness?*
> —Romans 6:16

> *If anyone teaches otherwise and does not consent to wholesome words, even the words of our Lord Jesus Christ, and to the doctrine which accords with godliness, he is proud, knowing nothing, but is obsessed with disputes and arguments over words, from which come envy, strife, reviling, evil suspicions, useless wranglings of men of corrupt minds and destitute of the truth, who suppose that godliness is a means of gain. From such withdraw yourself.*
> —1 Timothy 6:3-5

---

[18] *The New Strong's Exhaustive Concordance of the Bible*, James Strong's LL.D., S.T.D. Nashville, TN, by Thomas Nelson Publishers, 1990.

The Greek meaning of gain (por-is-mos') is a way, means, furnishing (procuring), money-getting (acquisition).[19]

To stand against this type of temptation, you must do as stated in Galatians:

> *I say then: Walk in the Spirit and you shall not fulfill the lust of the flesh. For the flesh lusts against the Spirit, and the Spirit against the flesh; and these are contrary to one another, so that you do not do the things that you wish.*
> —Galatians 5:16-17

Walking in the Spirit is a daily fight, but the Holy Spirit is your helper. You must be willing to keep at it to defeat your flesh and Satan.

Read the case Paul made about this fight in Romans 7:14-25.

_____

_____

_____

The answer to his case is found in the next chapter.

> *There is therefore now no condemnation to those who are in Christ Jesus, who do not walk according to the flesh, but according to the Spirit. For the law of the Spirit of life in Christ Jesus has made me free from the law of sin and death.*
> —Romans 8:1-2

---

[19] Ibid.

Revelations of God's Love

The decision to serve a master — God or money — is your personal responsibility. Since you cannot serve two masters, you must choose one.

Love leaves the choice up to you.

Gail P. Miller

Revelations of God's Love

Lesson 5 Questions

1. Is God saying that you cannot be rich and serve Him?
2. Is the love in 1 Timothy 6:10 the same as agapé love in John 3:16?
3. Do money, mammon, and gain have similar meanings?
4. How many masters can you serve?
5. What does godliness mean?
6. Are your flesh and spirit in agreement?
7. Are the treasures that you love tied to your heart?

Suggested materials to make the lesson come alive!
- To study the verses in context, read the entire chapters for Scriptures noted in the lesson. Use a Bible commentary like *Halley's Bible Handbook* or *Liberty Bible Commentary, The Old-Time Gospel Hour Edition*.
- Create a PowerPoint presentation adding your choice of images with each teaching point of the lesson.
- Make a poster of a tree with roots and leaves. Have students write evil words on the leaves or around the tree as a visual of how evil looks. Encourage students to define root. Remind students that "The love of money is the root of all evil," not money itself.
- Make posters of Scriptures to hang on the wall, easel, or bulletin board. Make copies for each student.

Gail P. Miller

Memory Verse

For the love of money is a root of all kinds of evil, for which some have strayed from the faith in their greediness, and pierced themselves through with many sorrows.
—1 Timothy 6:10

Lesson 5 Answers

The following answers are based on the lesson Scriptures and understanding of the subject matter. Because God's Word is alive, some questions may have answers beyond the ones provided here.

The Love of Money!

1. No. God is saying that if you love money/riches more than Him, you cannot love and serve Him. Whomever, or whatever, you serve dictates your actions, intentions, and motives. Exodus 20:3; Matthew 6:33
2. No.
3. Yes.
4. One.
5. Godliness (2150, Greek yoo-seb'-i-ah) piety, the gospel scheme: holiness.[20]
6. No. Galatians 5:17
7. Yes. Matthew 6:21

---

[20] *The New Strong's Exhaustive Concordance of the Bible*, James Strong's LL.D., S.T.D. Nashville, TN, by Thomas Nelson Publishers, 1990.

Gail P. Miller

Lesson 6
Love Chastens

Like a parent corrects a child to teach them right from wrong, love chastens, rebukes, and scourges you to redirect you to His will.

> *My son, do not despise the <u>chastening</u> of the Lord, nor detest His correction: For whom the Lord loves He corrects, just as a father the son in whom he delights.*
> —Proverbs 3:11-12

> *And you have forgotten the <u>exhortation</u> which speaks to you as to sons: My son, do not despise the <u>chastening</u> of the Lord, nor be discouraged when you are <u>rebuked</u> by Him; For whom the Lord loves He <u>chastens</u>, and <u>scourges</u> every son whom He receives.*
> —Hebrews 12:5-6

The following Greek definitions help illuminate the meaning of the above Scriptures:

- <u>Exhortation</u> (3874, Greek, par-ak'-lay-sis): to call near, invite, imploration, exhortation, solace: comfort, consolation, entreaty
- <u>Chastening</u> (3809, Greek, pahee di-ah): tutorage, education or training, disciplinary correction: chastening, chastisement, instruction, nurture

- <u>Rebuked</u> (1651, Greek, el-eng'kho): to confute, admonish; convict, convince, tell a fault, reprove
- <u>Chastens</u> (3811, Greek, pahee-dyoo'-o): to train up a child, educate, or discipline (by punishment): chasten (-ise), instruct, learn, teach
- <u>Scourges</u> (3146, Greek, mas-tig-o'-o): to flog, beat with a whip or stick as punishment or torture; whip, scourge, flagellate lash, switch, cane thrash, tan someone's hide.[21]

In Proverbs 3:11, the Hebrew meaning of <u>chastening</u> (moo-sawr') is chastisement, reproof, warning, or instruction; restraint; bond chastening ([-eth]), check, correction, discipline, doctrine, rebuke, 3256 (with blows or words)[22], reform.

Read this verse with the definitions inserted for a better understanding.

> *And you have forgotten the <u>invitation</u> which speaks to you as to sons: My son, do not despise the <u>education or training</u> of the Lord, nor be discouraged when you are <u>told your faults</u> by Him; For whom the Lord loves He <u>disciplines</u>, and <u>tans the hide</u> of every son whom He receives.*
> —Hebrews 12:5-6

Why does Love (God) do this to His children?

---

[21] *The New Strong's Exhaustive Concordance of the Bible,* James Strong's LL.D., S.T.D. Nashville, TN, by Thomas Nelson Publishers, 1990.
[22] Ibid.

> *If you endure <u>chastening or nurturing</u>, God deals with you as with sons; for what son is there whom a father does not <u>chasten or teach</u>? But if you are without <u>chastening or instruction</u>, of which all have become partakers, then you are <u>illegitimate</u> and not sons.*
> —Hebrews 12:7-8

In this scripture, the Greek meanings of "illegitimate" (noth'-os) is a <u>spurious</u> son, bastard.[23]

<u>Spurious</u> means having the appearance of being genuine, but without being so, false (artificial, pretend, fake-counterfeit, sham, and to deceive).[24]

Substituting <u>illegitimate</u> with its meaning, Hebrews 12:8 reads:

> *"But if you are without chastening or nurturing, of which all have become partakers, then you are* <u>having the appearance of being genuine, but without being so, false (artificial, pretend, fake-counterfeit, sham, and to deceive)</u>, *and not sons.*

To shed further light on why love (God) does this to His children, read the following verses:

---

[23] *The New Strong's Exhaustive Concordance of the Bible,* James Strong's LL.D., S.T.D. Nashville, TN, by Thomas Nelson Publishers, 1990.
[24] *The New Lexicon Webster's Dictionary of the English Language,* Encyclopedic Edition, Lexicon Publications, Inc. New York. 1989 Edition.

Furthermore, we have had human fathers who corrected us, and we paid them respect. Shall we not much more readily be in subjection to the Father of spirits and live? For they indeed for a few days chastened us as seemed best to them, but He for our profit (benefit) that we may be partakers of <u>His holiness</u>. Now no chastening seems to be joyful for the present, but painful; nevertheless, afterward it yields the <u>peaceable fruit of righteousness</u> to those who have been trained by it.
—Hebrews 12:9-11

<u>Pursue peace</u> with all people, and <u>holiness</u>, without which <u>no one will see the Lord</u>: looking carefully lest anyone fall short of the grace of God; lest any <u>root of bitterness</u> spring up cause trouble, and by this <u>many become defiled.</u>
—Hebrews 12:14-15

Regardless of race, age, or gender, everyone has to be corrected by God to see His face in peace.

Will you accept Love's invitation for correction?

Revelations of God's Love

Lesson 6 Questions

1. Why is it important to God for His children to endure His training and correction?
2. What is the result of the correction?

Suggested materials to make the lesson come alive!
- To study the verses in context, read the entire chapters for Scriptures noted in the lesson. Use a Bible commentary like *Halley's Bible Handbook* or *Liberty Bible Commentary, The Old-Time Gospel Hour Edition*.
- Create a PowerPoint presentation adding your choice of images with each teaching point of the lesson.
- Make posters of Scriptures to hang on the wall, easel, or bulletin board. Make copies for each student.

Memory Verse

But if you are without <u>chastening</u>, of which all have become partakers, then you are <u>illegitimate</u> and not sons.
—Hebrews 12:8

Gail P. Miller

Revelations of God's Love

Lesson 6 Answers

The following answers are based on the lesson Scriptures and understanding of the subject matter. Because God's Word is alive, some questions may have answers beyond the ones provided here.

Love Chastens!

1. So you can partake of God's holiness and bring forth the peaceable fruit of righteousness. Otherwise, a root of bitterness can spring up causing trouble and defilement.
2. Holiness, peace, and the grace of God. Without them, you cannot see the Lord.

Gail P. Miller

Revelations of God's Love

Lesson 7
No Boundaries

This lesson looks at <u>boundaries</u> as they relate to God's love. Paul revealed his understanding of the Unknown God to the great philosophers of Athens and Greece.[25]

> *God, who made the world and everything in it, since He is Lord of heaven and earth, does not dwell in temples made with hands. Nor is He worshiped with men's hands, as though He needed anything, since He gives to all life, breath, and all things. And He has made from one blood every nation of men to dwell on all the face of the earth, and has determined their pre-appointed times and the <u>boundaries</u> of their dwellings.*
> — Acts 17:24-26

The Greek meanings for bounds/boundaries (hor-oth-es-ee'-ah) are limit, a limit-placing, boundary-line, bound.[26]

In the previous Scriptures, God lets you know that He set boundaries for mankind. Does love have boundaries? Search the Scriptures to find evidence and results of this truth.

---

[25] *Liberty Bible Commentary, The Old Time Gospel Hour Edition,* Jerry Falwell, D.D., D. Litt. Edward E. Hindson, Th.D., D.Min., Woodrow Michael Knoll, Th.D.; Lynchburg, VA, 1983, pp. 2174-2175.

[26] *The New Strong's Exhaustive Concordance of the Bible,* James Strong's LL.D., S.T.D. Nashville, TN, Thomas Nelson Publishers, 1990.

Great is the Lord, and greatly to be praised; And His greatness is <u>unsearchable</u>.
—Psalm 145:3

Oh, the depth of the riches both of the wisdom and knowledge of God! How <u>unsearchable</u> are His judgments and His ways past finding out.
—Romans 11:33

To me, who am less than the least of all saints, this grace was given, that I should preach among the Gentiles the <u>unsearchable</u> riches of Christ.
—Ephesians 3:8

Other Old Testament Scriptures include the word unsearchable. Can you find some?

_____

_____

_____

These Scriptures confirm that the depth of the knowledge of Love cannot be fully comprehended. In these New Testament verses:
- <u>Unsearchable</u> (419, Greek an-ex-er-yoo'-nay-tos) means not searched out, unsearchable, and <u>inscrutable</u>[27]
- <u>Unsearchable</u> (421, Greek an-ex-ikh-nee'-as-tos) means not tracked out, past finding out.[28]

---

[27] *The New Strong's Exhaustive Concordance of the Bible,* James Strong's LL.D., S.T.D. Nashville, TN, Thomas Nelson Publishers, 1990.
[28] Ibid.

Revelations of God's Love

- <u>Inscrutable</u>: of such a kind that the meaning or intention cannot be perceived (to become aware of by understanding, discerned).[29]

Love can be your father, mother, or friend. I invite you to define who God is to you and find at least two Scriptures that confirm it.

_____

_____

_____

You serve the infinite, everlasting, limitless, immeasurable, <u>unsearchable</u>, inexhaustible, all-things-possible God!

---

[29] *The New Lexicon Webster's Dictionary of The English Language*, Encyclopedic Edition, Lexicon Publications, Inc. New York 1989, 1987.

Gail P. Miller

Revelations of God's Love

Lesson 7 Questions

Create your own questions for this lesson.

_____
_____
_____
_____
_____
_____
_____

Suggested materials to make the lesson come alive!
- To study the verses in context, read the entire chapters for Scriptures noted in the lesson. Use a Bible commentary like *Halley's Bible Handbook* or *Liberty Bible Commentary, The Old-Time Gospel Hour Edition*.
- Create a PowerPoint presentation adding your choice of images with each teaching point of the lesson.
- Make posters of Scriptures to hang on the wall, easel, or bulletin board. Make copies for each student.

Memory Verse

> *Oh, the depth of the riches both of the wisdom and knowledge of God! How unsearchable are His judgments and His ways past finding out.*
> —Romans 11:33

Gail P. Miller

Revelations of God's Love

Lesson 7 Answers

Base your answers on the Scriptures provided in the lesson and personal understanding related to the subject matter.

No Boundaries!

_____
_____
_____
_____
_____
_____
_____

Old Testament Scriptures containing unsearchable (See page 76) include Job 5:9 and Proverbs 25:3.

Gail P. Miller

Lesson 8
Love Defeated the Real Bully

A bully is someone who enjoys oppressing others weaker than himself, to persecute physically or spiritually, or to intimidate or force.[30] The first step to defeat the "real bully" is knowing that one exists.

God declared what he was going to do to this bully.

> *And I will put enmity between you and the woman, and between your seed and her Seed; He shall bruise your head, and you shall bruise His heel.*
> —Genesis 3:15

Jesus said,

> *The thief does not come except to <u>steal</u> and to <u>kill</u> and to <u>destroy</u>, I have come that they may have life, and that they may have it more abundantly.*
> —John 10:10

Review these definitions to gain wisdom, knowledge, and understanding of how this bully operates:

---

[30] *The New Lexicon Webster's Dictionary of The English Language*, Encyclopedic Edition, Lexicon Publications, Inc. New York 1989, 1987.

- <u>Steal</u> (2813, Greek klep'-to) to filch;[31] steal. <u>Filch</u>- pilfer, take for oneself, help oneself to, loot, carry off, swipe, snatch, nab, rip off, rob, shoplift, lift[32]
- <u>Kill</u> (2380; Greek thoo'-o) to rush (breath hard, blow, smoke), to sacrifice, to immolate (slaughter for any purpose); kill, (do) sacrifice, slay
- <u>Destroy</u> (622; Greek ap-ol'-loo-mee) to destroy fully, to perish, or lose, die, mar; impair the appearance of, disfigure, spoil, scar, mutilate, deface, deform, ruin, wreck, harm, damage, hurt, stain, pollute, blemish, tarnish, blight[33]

Now that you know what this bully does, you need to know what methods he uses, where these battles occur, and the realm from which this bully works.

> *For we do not wrestle against flesh and blood, but against principalities, against powers, against the rulers of the darkness of this age, against spiritual host of wickedness in the heavenly places.*
> – Ephesians 6: 12

This verse reveals that your fight is not against people or things in the natural realm, but with supernatural beings in heavenly places and on Earth. As you battle these beings with the Word of Truth and the name of Jesus, Satan and his

---

[31] *The New Strong's Exhaustive Concordance of the Bible,* James Strong's LL.D., S.T.D. Nashville, TN, Thomas Nelson Publishers, 1990.
[32] *The New Lexicon Webster's Dictionary of The English Language,* Encyclopedic Edition, Lexicon Publications, Inc. New York 1989, 1987.
[33] *The New Strong's Exhaustive Concordance of the Bible,* James Strong's LL.D., S.T.D. Nashville, TN, Thomas Nelson Publishers, 1990.

army wage warfare against your mind, the first battle ground.

> *For to be carnally* (natural) *minded is death, but to be spiritually minded is life and peace. Because the carnal mind is enmity* (an enemy) *against God; for it is not subject to the law of God, nor indeed can be.*
> —Romans 8:6-7

For this reason, Satan attacks your mind to construct strongholds that cause you to fight against God with your reasoning, imaginations, and understandings (1 Corinthians 10:4-6). Measure your thoughts and what Satan says to you with what God says. If you decide to respond to what pleases your eyes, flesh, and/or pride then, Satan has you in his grip (Proverbs 3:5-7; Romans 8:1-5; 1 John 2:16).

Go to the beginning to see how this fight started. Read and discuss Genesis 1:26-27; 2:7-8, 15-17.

_____

_____

_____

Compare these verses with Genesis 2:16-17 and Genesis 3:1-6.

> *And the Lord God commanded the man, saying, "Of every tree of the garden you may freely eat; but of the tree of the knowledge of good and evil you shall not eat, for in the day that you eat of it you shall surely die."*
> —Genesis 2:16-17

Now the serpent was more cunning than any beast of the field which the Lord God had made. And he said to the woman, "Has God indeed said, '<u>You</u> shall not eat of every tree of the garden?' And the woman said to the serpent, "We may eat the fruit of the trees of the garden; but of the fruit of the tree which is in the midst of the garden, God has said, '<u>You</u> shall not eat it, nor shall <u>you</u> touch it, lest <u>you</u> die.'" Then the <u>serpent said</u> to the woman, "<u>You</u> will not surely die. For God knows that in the day <u>you</u> eat of it <u>your</u> eyes will be opened, and <u>you</u> will be like God, knowing good and evil." So when the woman saw that the tree was good for food, that it was pleasant to the eyes, and a tree desirable to make one wise, she took of its fruit and ate. She also gave to her husband with her, and he ate.
—Genesis 3:1-6

This method of casting doubt on what God said while appealing to what you want is a common tactic of Satan. Adam and Eve were already like God having been made in His image. They had direct access to ask Him anything and as the Creator of everything, He had all the answers.

Adam was charged with tending and keeping the garden of Eden in Genesis 2:15. In this verse, keep is defined as follows:

<u>Keep</u> (8104, Hebrew shaw-mar') to hedge about (as with thorns), guard, to protect, attend to, beware, be circumspect, take heed (to self), keep (-er, self), mark, look narrowly,

observe, preserve, regard, reserve, save (self), sure, (that lay) wait (for), watch(-man).[34]

Satan was already on Earth.

Therefore rejoice, O heavens, and you who dwell in them! Woe to the inhabitants of the earth and the sea! For the devil has come down to you, having great wrath because he knows that he has a short time.

—Revelation 12:12

Read Genesis 1:28 to see what Adam should have done based on God's instruction. Compare that verse to what Jesus said in Matthew 4:1-11 and Luke 4:1-13 to understand what you are to do now.

_____

_____

_____

God had already commanded Adam to take dominion over every living thing that moved on Earth. Jesus, who is the Word, spoke what His Father wrote in Matthew 4 and Luke 4. The Holy Spirit was with Jesus when this tempting occurred. Satan changed his plan of attack three times and misquoted God's Word to the Word in an attempt to deceive Christ. These temptations were unsuccessful; however, you must understand the importance of knowing what is written. You have to speak His Word out loud to Satan and his demonic forces. It is your responsibility to study, know, and obey God's Word. If you are filled with the Holy Spirit,

---

[34]*The New Strong's Exhaustive Concordance of the Bible*, James Strong's LL.D., S.T.D. Nashville, TN, Thomas Nelson Publishers, 1990.

you can call on Him for help. One of His names is Helper (John 14:26). The outcome for Adam, Eve, and mankind would have been different had they taken their dominion and spoken God's Word.

Since the Word of God is your weapon, read what the Word says about your sword.

> *For the Word of God is living and powerful, and sharper than any two-edged sword, piercing even to the <u>division</u> of soul and spirit, and of joints and marrow, and is a discerner of the thoughts and intents of the <u>heart</u>.*
> — Hebrews 4: 12

Read what Jesus did to this bully and his armies in Colossians 2:15 and Luke 10:18-20. He rendered them powerless in heaven and on Earth. This bully is powerless over you, too.

> *Having <u>disarmed</u> <u>principalities</u> and <u>powers</u>, he made a <u>public</u> <u>spectacle</u> of them, <u>triumphing</u> over them in it.*
> —Colossians 2:15

I separated this Scripture into two parts to define the underlined words.

Part 1: Having <u>disarmed</u> <u>principalities</u> and <u>powers</u>, Jesus disarmed:
- spoiled
- put off

- divested or stripped[35]
- to cut down armaments or weapons
- deprive or take away the power to harm[36]

Who? Principalities.
- chief, of order, time, place or rank
- first (estate)
- magistrate, power
- principle, rule

What? Powers.
- ability, privilege, force
- capacity, competency, freedom, mastery
- magistrate, superhuman, potentate (1 Timothy 6:15), token of control
- delegated influence
- authority, jurisdiction, liberty
- power, right, strength

Part 2: He made a public spectacle of them, triumphing over them in it.

Jesus made a public:[37]
- public, publicly
- openly, people, common

Jesus made a shew/spectacle[38]:
- to exhibit
- to display (openly)
- make a show

---

[35] *The New Strong's Exhaustive Concordance of the Bible*, James Strong's LL.D., S.T.D. Nashville, TN, Thomas Nelson Publishers, 1990.
[36] *The New Lexicon Webster's Dictionary of The English Language*, Encyclopedic Edition, Lexicon Publications, Inc. New York 1989, 1987.
[37] *The New Strong's Exhaustive Concordance of the Bible*, James Strong's LL.D., S.T.D. Nashville, TN, Thomas Nelson Publishers, 1990.
[38] Ibid.

- a specimen or example (of publicly) Jesus triumphing:[39]
  - a noisy song
  - to make an acclamatory or enthusiastic procession
  - to conquer
  - to give victory, cause to triumph over

The Lord wants you to understand that Satan, the devil, is not a lion nor does he have the roar of a lion. Because of Jesus's death, burial, and resurrection, the devil is defeated and pretends to be like a roaring lion. His imitation is designed to put fear in you and trick you into believing that he has authority over you (1 Peter 5:8).

<u>Pretend</u> is to allege falsely (a false impression) go through the motions, lay claim to (some honor, quality etc.)[40]

<u>As/Like</u> (5613, Greek hoce) in that manner, it was, and even as.[41]

In Luke 10:18, Jesus said, "I saw Satan fall like lighting from heaven." Read Revelation 12:1-17 for more about the defeat of the fallen angel.

_____

_____

_____

---

[39] Ibid.

[40] *The New Lexicon Webster's Dictionary of The English Language*, Encyclopedic Edition, Lexicon Publications, Inc. New York 1989, 1987.

[41] *The New Strong's Exhaustive Concordance of the Bible*, James Strong's LL.D., S.T.D. Nashville, TN, Thomas Nelson Publishers, 1990.

> *Behold, I give <u>you</u> the <u>authority</u> to <u>trample</u> on <u>serpents</u> and <u>scorpions</u>, and over <u>all the power</u> of the <u>enemy</u>, and nothing shall by any means hurt <u>you</u>.*
> —Luke 10:19

<u>Authority</u> is power, privilege, force or freedom.[42]
<u>Trample</u> means to tread down or under foot (Read 2 Corinthians 5:7 and 10:4-7).[43]
<u>Serpents</u> are snakes, Satan
<u>Scorpions</u> can sting or pierce
<u>Power</u> is abilities, might, or violence
<u>Enemy</u> means adversary, hateful acts[44]

Recall Genesis 3:15 where God said that He put hostility between Satan and the woman. Jesus declared:

> *Nevertheless* (or in spite of that) *do not rejoice in this, <u>that the spirits are subject to you</u> but* (rather) *rejoice because your names are <u>written</u> in heaven.*
> —Luke 10:20

Meditate on the fact that demonic spirits are subject to you. Acknowledge that your name is written in heaven.

<u>Written</u> (1125, Greek graf-o) to grave or engrave, to write, to <u>describe</u>, write (-ing,-ten).[45]

---

[42] Ibid.
[43] *The New Strong's Exhaustive Concordance of the Bible*, James Strong's LL.D., S.T.D. Nashville, TN, Thomas Nelson Publishers, 1990.
[44] *The New Strong's Exhaustive Concordance of the Bible*, James Strong's LL.D., S.T.D. Nashville, TN, Thomas Nelson Publishers, 1990.
[45] Ibid.

<u>Describe</u> means to give a description of, to qualify, to draw, trace, to move in the outline of.[46]

Your name was written, described, or engraved on the books of heaven by the hand of God when you got saved (Revelation 20:12). Jesus sits at the right hand of God, the seat of power. The Lord keeps a running tab, account, and catalog of your life.

So, how did your name get engraved in heaven? Morse code, special delivery, or a message in a bottle? You already know. Jesus!

Jesus provides a counterattack to the enemy's plans.

> *The thief does not come except to steal and to kill and to destroy, I have come that they may <u>have life</u>, and that they may <u>have it more abundantly</u>.*
> —John 10:10

The enemy of your soul wants carnal thoughts to get into your heart so you speak them aloud and act on them. (Proverbs 18:21; Matthew 12:34; Colossians 3:16).

_____

_____

_____

The real bully came to steal your faith, kill your hopes, and to destroy you, but love said that he is a liar and the father of lies (John 8:44). Love came to give you abundant,

---

[46] *The New Lexicon Webster's Dictionary of The English Language*, Encyclopedic Edition, Lexicon Publications, Inc. New York 1989, 1987.

eternal life including power over Satan. However, if you don't obey His Word, then all this understanding is moot.

Walk in the victory love gave you because…love won!

Gail P. Miller

Revelations of God's Love

Lesson 8 Questions

1. Who is the real bully?
2. Where is spiritual warfare waged?
3. How do you engage this bully?
4. What common method does Satan use to get you not to believe God?
5. Does Satan have authority over God's people?

Suggested materials to make the lesson come alive!
- Read the following chapters for further understanding of the victory you have in this fight. Job 1:6-12, 2:1-7; Proverbs 18:21; Ephesians 6:11-18.
- To study the verses in context, read the entire chapters for Scriptures noted in the lesson. Use a Bible commentary like *Halley's Bible Handbook* or *Liberty Bible Commentary, The Old-Time Gospel Hour Edition*.
- Create a PowerPoint presentation adding your choice of images with each teaching point of the lesson.
- Make posters of Scriptures to hang on the wall, easel, or bulletin board. Make copies for each student.
- Encourage students to discuss previous forms of delivery and communication including smoke signals, carrier pigeons, and pony express.
- Compare that list to current forms of delivery and communication like smart phones, social media, and television. Discuss how to communicate with God and ways He communicates with you.

Gail P. Miller

Memory Verse

Having disarmed principalities and powers, He made a public spectacle of them, triumphing over them in it.
—Colossians 2:15

Revelations of God's Love

Lesson 8 Answers

The following answers are based on the lesson Scriptures and understanding of the subject matter. Because God's Word is alive, some questions may have answers beyond the ones provided here.

Love Defeated the Real Bully!

1. Satan, his demons, and his wicked forces.
2. In our minds so He can plant His Word in our hearts, too.
3. With your spiritual weapon, the Word of Truth, the name of Jesus, prayer, praise, and worship.
4. Deceiving you to doubt God's Word. If you know His Word, Satan will twist it to get you to use it in error. If you don't know God's Word, then you become his victim.
5. No, but you have to know that he doesn't.

Gail P. Miller

Revelations of God's Love

Lesson 9
Your Example

Since love is your example, read what the Lord said about mankind when He made us.

Then God said, "Let us make man in our image, according to our likeness."
—Genesis 1:26a

Because you are made in His likeness, you should be like, act like, and look like them. Based on what the Father said, "Our image and our likeness," He created you to resemble the Father, the Son, and the Holy Ghost…them.

These Hebrew meanings help illuminate your understanding:
- <u>Image</u> (tseh'-lem) resemblance, a representative, figure
- <u>Likeness</u> (dem-ooth') resemblance, model, shape, fashion, manner, similitude

You are made according to His kind. In the following verses, witness how Jesus expressed servitude and love to His disciples:

If then, your Lord and teacher, has washed your feet, you also ought to wash one another's feet. For I have given you an <u>example</u>, that you should do as I have done to you.
—John 13:14-15

Example means:
- (5262, Greek hoop-od'-igue-mah) an exhibit for imitation or warning, pattern, instruct, to show (John 13:15; James 5:10)
- (5179, Greek too'-pos); a die (as struck), a stamp, a shape, style or resemblance, a sampler, type, a model, (for warning), print, manner (1 Timothy 4:12)
- (5261, Greek hoop-og-ram-mos') an underwriting, copy for imitation, example (1 Peter 2:21)
- (1164, Greek digh'-mah) a specimen (as shown): example[47] (Jude 7)

After the Passover supper, Jesus washed the feet of His disciples, a duty of slaves. Christ made an example (exhibit for imitation or a model) for the disciples to position themselves as servants and not rulers. Jesus settled their dispute about who would be the greatest in God's kingdom. He showed His disciple how to be humble. He warned them about the spirit of pride.[48] (Matthew 18:4; James 4:6; 1 Peter 5:5-6)

---

[47] *The New Strong's Exhaustive Concordance of the Bible*, James Strong's LL.D., S.T.D. Nashville, TN, Thomas Nelson Publishers, 1990.
[48] *Halley's Bible Handbook with The New International Version*, Zondervan, Grand Rapids, MI 2000 pp. 703-704.

Revelations of God's Love

To develop an understanding of your life as a disciple of Jesus, read these verses. Synonyms were added for clarity.

> *"Let no one despise your youth, but be an example (a type, model, or warning) to the believers in word, in conduct, in love, in spirit, in faith, in purity."*
> —1 Timothy 4:12

Paul wrote to Timothy, his spiritual son, on how to successfully handle apostasy and people problems with God as the foundation. Timothy resembled Christ as he followed the leading of the Holy Spirit.[49]

> *Let us therefore be diligent to enter that rest, lest anyone fall according to the same example (exhibit or pattern) of disobedience. For the Word of God is living and powerful, and shaper than any two-edged sword, piercing even to the division of soul and spirit, and of joints and marrow, and is a discerner of the thoughts and intents of the heart.*
> —Hebrews 4:11-12

> *For what credit is it if, when you are beaten for your faults, you take it patiently? But when you do good and <u>suffer</u>, if you take it patiently, this is commendable before God. For to this you were called, because Christ also suffered for us, leaving*

---

[49] *New Spirit Filled Life Bible*, Jack W. Hayford, Li.D., Paul G. Chappell, Ph.D., Kenneth C. Ulmer, Ph. D., D.Min., Roy Hayden, Ph. D., Jonathan David Huntzinger, Ph. D., Gary Matsdorf, M.A., Thomas Nelson Bible, 2002, pp.1699-1700.

us an example (a copy for imitation or a stamp), *that you should follow His steps: Who committed no sin, Nor was <u>deceit</u> found in His mouth; who, when He was <u>reviled</u>, did not revile in return; when He suffered, He did not <u>threaten</u>, but <u>committed</u> Himself to Him who judge righteously.*
—1 Peter 2:20-23

These are the definitions for the underlined words in theses verses:

- <u>Suffer</u> (3958, Greek pas'-kho); to experience a sensation (painful): feel, vex[50]
- <u>Deceit/Guile</u> (1388, Greek dol'-os) wile: craft, trick (bate) to entrap
- <u>Reviled</u> (486, Greek an-tee-lay-dor-eh'-o) to rail in reply, to reproach, vilify
- <u>Threaten</u> (546, Greek ap-i-leh'-o) to menace; (be hostile, frighten, bully) to forbid
- <u>Committed</u> (3860, Greek par-ad-id-o-mee) to surrender, yield up, in trust, transmit: betray, bring forth, cast deliver (up), give (over, up), hazard, put in prison, recommend[51]

Jesus displayed that you will suffer for the gospel's sake. Do not try to entrap people with your words or rail at them when they vilify you. You are not to threaten others when they are hostile toward you. This action—or lack thereof—may seem unfair, but it is the will of God.

---

[50] *The New Strong's Exhaustive Concordance of the Bible*, James Strong's LL.D., S.T.D. Nashville, TN, Thomas Nelson Publishers, 1990.
[51] Ibid.

Revelations of God's Love

Some leaders had abandoned the teaching of Christ in the churches in Asia Minor. Jude wrote them a stern warning with a long list of errors, heresies, and sexually immoral acts that needed urgent correction. He reiterated to these churches what was said about the last days. He warned them to be aware of false teachers whose goal was to destroy the church and overturn Christ's work on the cross.[52]

> *Beloved, while I was very diligent to write to you concerning our common salvation, I found it necessary to write to you exhorting you to contend earnestly for the faith which was once for all delivered to the saints. For certain men have crept in unnoticed who long ago were marked out for this condemnation, ungodly men who turn the grace of God into lewdness and deny the only Lord God and our Lord Jesus Christ. As Sodom and Gomorrah, and the cities around them in a similar manner to these, having given themselves over to sexual immorality and gone after strange flesh, are set forth as an example* (a specimen as show or a sample), *suffering the vengeance of eternal fire.*
> —Jude 3-4, 7

---

[52] *Halley's Bible Handbook with The New International Version*, Zondervan, Grand Rapids, MI, 2000 pp. 893-894

Gail P. Miller

This world is dark and sinful, but your hope is in Christ Jesus. Regardless of what others think, say, or do, as a child of light, you must reflect His light to illuminate the way for others. Therefore, your thoughts, words, and deeds will make all the difference if you live according to Christ's example, model, and pattern.

Is your life an example of Love?

Revelations of God's Love

Lesson 9 Questions

1. What does example mean?
2. Who is your example?
3. Is suffering a part of your walk with God?
4. If someone threatens you, how should you respond?
5. If a believer is not following the leading of the Holy Spirit, can that affect their example of Christ?

Suggested materials to make the lesson come alive!
- Read the following passages for further understanding of how to conduct yourself as a child of God: 1 Samuel 15:22-23; Psalm 25:9-10; Proverbs 11:2; Matthew 5:11-12; Romans 8:12-17, 12:19-21; 1 Corinthians 10:1-11; 2 Timothy 2: 3-7; Hebrews 10:30; James 1:19-25.
- To study the verses in context, read the entire chapters for Scriptures noted in the lesson. Use a Bible commentary like *Halley's Bible Handbook* or *Liberty Bible Commentary, The Old-Time Gospel Hour Edition*.
- Create a PowerPoint presentation adding your choice of images with each teaching point of the lesson.
- Make posters of Scriptures to hang on the wall, easel, or bulletin board. Make copies for each student.

Gail P. Miller

Memory Verse

For I have given you an <u>example</u>, that you should do as I have done to you.
—John 13:15

Lesson 9 Answers

The following answers are based on the lesson Scriptures and understanding of the subject matter. Because God's Word is alive, some questions may have answers beyond the ones provided here.

Your Example!

1. Read the meanings in the lesson to create its meaning to you.
2. Jesus. John 13:14-15
3. Yes. 1 Peter 2:20-23
4. Answers vary. 1 Peter 2:20-23
5. Yes. Romans 8:12-17

Gail P. Miller

Revelations of God's Love

Lesson 10
Living By Every Word

This lesson delves into what sustains you beyond natural food.

> *And you shall remember that the Lord your God led you all the way these forty years in the wilderness, to humble you and test you, to know what was in your heart, whether you would keep His commandments or not. So He humbled you, allowed you to hunger, and fed you with manna which you did not know nor did your fathers know, that He might make you know that man shall not live by bread alone; but man lives by <u>every word</u> that proceeds from the mouth of the Lord.*
> —Deuteronomy 8:2-3

The following Scriptures illustrate Satan's attempt to tempt Jesus after He had been in the wilderness for forty days without food.

> *Now when the tempter came to Him, he said, "If You are the Son of God, command that these stones become bread."*
> —Matthew 4:3

> *And the devil said to Him, "If You are the Son of God, command this stone to become bread."*
> —Luke 4:3

Despite the enemy's efforts, Christ did not yield. God's pleasure in His Son was expressed following His baptism by John.

> *And suddenly a voice came from heaven saying, "This is My beloved Son, in whom I am well pleased."*
> —Matthew 3:17

Christ often spoke of what it takes to live for Him.

> *But He answered and said, "It is <u>written</u>, <u>Man</u> shall not live by bread alone, but by every word that proceeds from the mouth of God."*
> —Matthew 4:4

> *But Jesus answered him, saying, "It is <u>written</u>, <u>Man</u> shall not live by bread alone, but by <u>every word</u> of God."*
> —Luke 4:4

- <u>Written</u> (1125, Greek graf'-o); to grave- (to shape by carving, fix permanently, engrave, to write, to describe: describe, write (-ing, ten)
- <u>Man</u> (444, Greek anth'-ro-pos): man-faced, a human being: certain, man
- <u>Every</u> (3956, Greek pas); all, any, every, the whole: all (manner of, means), alway (-s), any (one), x daily, + ever, ever (one, way), as many as, + no)-thing), x thoroughly, whatsoever, whosoever[53]

---

[53] *The New Strong's Exhaustive Concordance of the Bible,* James Strong's LL.D., S.T.D. Nashville, TN, Thomas Nelson Publishers, 1990.

- Word (4487, Greek hray'-mah) an utterance, a matter or topic (of narration, command or dispute) naught whatever: + evil, + nothing, saying, word[54]

God wants you to know that you are to live by whatever He says, written or spoken.

> *So He humbled you, allowed you to hunger, and fed you with manna which you did not know nor did your fathers know, that He might make you know that man shall not live by <u>bread alone; but man lives by every word that proceeds from the mouth of the Lord.</u>*
> – Deuteronomy 8:3 NKJV[55]

The following verse declares that Jesus, the Word, came from God and is God.

> *In the beginning was the Word, and the Word was with God, and the Word was God.*
> —John 1:1

When God speaks to you through His prophets or His written Word, Jesus echoes His Father's words.

---

[54] *The New Strong's Exhaustive Concordance of the Bible*, James Strong's LL.D., S.T.D. Nashville, TN, Thomas Nelson Publishers, 1990.

[55] *New Spirit Filled Life Bible*, Jack W. Hayford, Li. D., Paul G. Chappell, Ph.D., Kenneth C. Ulmer, Ph. D., D. Min., Roy Hayden, Ph. D., Jonathan David Huntzinger, Ph. D., Gary Matsdorf, M.A., Thomas Nelson Bible, 2002.

> *"He who does not love Me does not keep My Word; and the word which you hear is not Mine but the Father's who sent Me."*
> —John 14:24

Jesus admonished the Jews who wanted to kill Him for breaking the Sabbath and making Himself equal to God.

> *Then Jesus answered and said to them, "Most assuredly, I say to you, the Son can do nothing of Himself, but what He sees the Father do; for whatever He does, the Son also does in like manner."*
> —John 5:19

Review what Jesus said about Himself in John 6 specifically verses 27, 32-33, 35, 38, 41b, 48-51, 55-58.

_____
_____
_____

These characteristics of Christ are necessary for you to understand the standard by which He wants you to live. Your life's source is His every Word. Your salvation and life are wrapped up in this food and drink that come directly from Him. The following definitions are the Greek meanings of these New Testament words:

- <u>Bread</u> (ar'-tos); bread (as raised) or a loaf: (shew-) bread, from 142, to lift, to take up or away, to raise (the voice) by Hebrew, [comp. 5375] to expiate sin:

away with, carry, loose, remove, bear (up), help, pardon
- Food/Meat (bro'-sis); eating, food, meat, to eat
- Manna (man'nah); an edible gum, man, of Hebrew (4478); a whatness or (what is it)
- Blood (hah'ee-mah); blood of men or animal, (the atoning blood of Christ); kindred; blood
- Drink (pee'-no); to imbibe: consume or sub, drink, and (pos-ak'-is); how many times: how oft (-en); (who, what)[56]

As you study the Old Testament, you'll discover that the children of Israel complained to Moses and Aaron about not having food as they wandered in the wilderness. Exodus Chapter 16 describes when the children of Israel first saw manna. God fed them "living bread" every day for forty years. They collected food every morning except the Sabbath. Does this sound familiar? Every day seeking Him, reading your Bible, and doing what God says to you.

Read Deuteronomy 28:1-14, 45, 58-59 to see how living by — or not living by — God's Word affects you. Focus on *if you* and the phrases that follow. If you choose not to obey His Word, then you need to know the consequences. Like Adam and Eve were cast out of the garden for making a bad choice, disobedience has penalties.

In the Hebrew, *if* means conditional particle, in case that, provided, when (-so ever), except or possibility. Other

---

[56] *The New Strong's Exhaustive Concordance of the Bible,* **James Strong's LL.D., S.T.D. Nashville, TN, Thomas Nelson Publishers, 1990.**

meanings are until, unless, since, or yet. Therefore, "if" is mainly a conditional word.[57]

Read these Scriptures to know how God's blessings come to you. Genesis 4:7; Exodus 19:5; 2 Chronicles 7:13-14; 1 Samuel 15:22-23; Matthew 5:43-48; John 15:10 to reinforce how God's blessings come upon you.

_____

_____

_____

_____

_____

_____

_____

> *Now it shall come to pass, (in case that, provided that, until, unless, or when so ever) you <u>diligently</u> obey the voice of the Lord your God, to observe carefully all His commandments which I command you today that the Lord your God will set you high above all nations of the earth. And all these blessings shall come upon you and overtake you, because you obey the voice of the Lord your God.*
> —Deuteronomy 28:1-2

The first two verses in Deuteronomy 28 set the stage to see the benefits you will receive when you obey God's Word. The next twelve verses demonstrate the promises; however, verses 16 through 68 uncover a flood of curses that God

---

[57] *The New Strong's Exhaustive Concordance of the Bible*, James Strong's LL.D., S.T.D. Nashville, TN, Thomas Nelson Publishers, 1990.

threatened to bring upon those who disobey. The Old Testament is the shadow of things to come as the punishment for Israel's sin was immediate. Now, by Christ's shed blood on the cross, grace and mercy will give us time before punishment. Blessings and curses are real, and God's mercies are new every day depending upon <u>if you</u>.

> Blessings and curses are in your hands.
> Which will you live by?

Gail P. Miller

Revelations of God's Love

Lesson 10 Questions

1. What does written mean?
2. Can you get all of God's blessings without obedience even though God rains on the just and the unjust?
3. Who is the bread from heaven?
4. How do you eat this bread?
5. How is a Christian self-deceived or self-deluded?
6. Is it your responsibility to seek God daily?
7. How does a Christian have the kind of life Jesus died to give them? Circle the correct answer.
   a) By hearing the Word at church, on the radio, TV, or any other device.
   b) By singing and dancing to the Word of God.
   c) By memorizing the Word, talking about it, and praising Him for it.
   d) By being a hearer and doer of the Word.

Suggested materials to make the lesson come alive!
- Read John 4:31-34 and James 1:21-25 for more understanding of what food means and being a doer of the word.
- To study the verses in context, read the entire chapters for Scriptures noted in the lesson. Use a Bible commentary like *Halley's Bible Handbook* or *Liberty Bible Commentary, The Old-Time Gospel Hour Edition*.
- Create a PowerPoint presentation adding your choice of images with each teaching point of the lesson.
- Make posters of Scriptures to hang on the wall, easel, or bulletin board. Make copies for each student.

- Define words needed to clarify wisdom and understanding.

Memory Verse

But Jesus answered him, saying, "It is written, 'Man shall not live by bread alone, but by <u>every word</u> of God.'"
—Luke 4:4

Revelations of God's Love

Lesson 10 Answers

The following answers are based on the lesson Scriptures and understanding of the subject matter. Because God's Word is alive, some questions may have answers beyond the ones provided here.

Living by Every Word!

1. <u>Written</u> (1125, Greek graf'-o); to grave (to shape by carving, fix permanently, engrave, to write, to describe: describe, write (-ing, ten).[58]
2. No. Some blessings come with conditions.
3. Jesus!
4. By reading, studying, and doing His Word.
5. By not being a doer of the Word. James 1:22-25
6. Yes. It is your responsibility to seek God daily to see what He has to say to you and what He wants you to do. Luke 9:23
7. D. James 1:22

---

[58] *The New Strong's Exhaustive Concordance of the Bible*, James Strong's LL.D., S.T.D. Nashville, TN, Thomas Nelson Publishers, 1990.

Gail P. Miller

Revelations of God's Love

Love Notes

For God so loved the world that He gave His only begotten Son, that whoever believes in Him should not perish but have everlasting life.
—John 3:16

Gail P. Miller

Love's Mercy

Surely goodness and mercy shall follow me All the days of my life; And I will dwell in the house of the Lord Forever."
—Psalm 23:6

Have <u>mercy</u> upon me, O God, According to Your loving-kindness; According to the multitude of Your tender mercies, <u>Blot out my transgressions</u>.
—Psalm 51:1

I will sing of the mercies of the Lord forever; With my mouth will I make known Your faithfulness to all generation.
—Psalm 89:1

Through the Lord's mercies we are not consumed, Because His compassions fail not. They are new <u>every morning</u>; Great is Your faithfulness.
—Lamentations 3:22-23

Blessed are the merciful For they shall obtain mercy.
—Matthew 5:7

Through the <u>tender mercy</u> of our God, with which the Dayspring from on high has visited us.
—Luke 1:78

Therefore as the elect of God, holy and beloved, put on <u>tender mercies</u>, kindness, humility, meekness, longsuffering; bearing with one another, and

forgiving one another, if anyone has a complaint against another; even as Christ forgave you, so you also must do.
—Colossians 3:12-13

Mercy says, "Today is a new day!"

Revelations of God's Love

Love Transformed Himself for You

<u>Transfigured</u> (3339, Greek met-am-or-fo'-o) to transform, <u>metamorphose</u> change;⁵⁹ <u>Metamorphose</u> is to change into a different physical form, to change the appearance or character of, to undergo metamorphosis or a marked change, form, and structure.⁶⁰

>*And the Lord went before them by day in a <u>pillar of cloud</u> to lead the way, and by night in a <u>pillar of fire</u> to give them light, so as to go by day and night.*
>—Exodus 13:21

>*So he said, No but as <u>Commander of the army of the Lord</u> I have now come.*
>—Joshua 5:14a

>*The Lord is my <u>rock</u> and my fortress and my <u>deliver</u>, My God, my strength, in whom I will trust; My <u>shield</u> and the horn of my salvation, my <u>stronghold</u>.*
>—Psalm 18:2

>*"For My people have committed two evils: They have forsaken Me, the <u>fountain of</u> <u>living waters</u>, and hewn themselves cisterns-broken cisterns that can hold no water."*
>—Jeremiah 2:13

---

⁵⁹ *The New Strong's Exhaustive Concordance of the Bible*, **James Strong's** LL.D., S.T.D. Nashville, TN, Thomas Nelson Publishers, 1990.

⁶⁰ *The New Lexicon Webster's Dictionary of The English Language*, Encyclopedic Edition, Lexicon Publications, Inc. New York 1989, 1987.

And Jesus said to them, "I am the <u>bread of life</u>. He who comes to me shall never hunger, and he who believes in Me shall never thirst."
—John 6:35

I am the <u>door</u>. If anyone enters by Me, he will be saved, and will go in and out and find pasture. I am the <u>good shepherd</u>. The good shepherd gives His life for the sheep.
—John 10:9,11

Jesus said to her, "I am <u>the resurrection</u> and <u>the life</u>. He who believes in Me, though he may die, he shall live."
—John 11:25

Jesus said to him, 'I am <u>the way</u>, <u>the truth</u>, and <u>the life</u>. No one comes to the Father except through Me."
—John 14:6

<u>I am the true vine</u>, and My Father is the vinedresser. Every branch in Me that does not bear fruit He takes away, and every branch that bears fruit He prunes, that it may bear more fruit."
—John 15:1-2

I am the <u>Alpha</u> and the <u>Omega</u>, the <u>Beginning</u> and the <u>End</u>, says the Lord, who is and who was and who is to come, the Almighty.
—Revelations 1:8

Love did it all just for <u>you</u>!

Love's Comparisons

Use the following chart to determine whether you are led by the Spirit (Love) or your flesh.

Spirit	**Flesh**
I walk according to the Spirit.	I walk according to the flesh.
I set my mind on the things of the Spirit.	I set my mind on the things of the flesh.
I am spiritually minded.	I am carnally minded.
My mind is at peace with God.	My mind is hostel toward God.
The Spirit of God dwells in me.	The Spirit of God is not in me.
I walk by faith and not by sight.	I walk by my feelings and what I see.
I believe in His Son.	I don't believe in His Son.
I am filled with the Spirit.	I am filled with wine.
I take chastening from the Lord.	I don't take any chastening.
I am a doer of the word.	I am a hearer only.
I have sex only with my spouse.	I have sex outside of marriage.
I get angry, but do not sin.	I get angry and sin.
I do not avenge myself.	I seek vengeance.
I forgive.	I hold unforgiveness.
I bridle my tongue.	I say what I want.
When I sin, I confess it.	When I sin, I hide it.

Gail P. Miller

Whose side are <u>you</u> on?

<u>Scriptures</u>
Psalm 4:4; Proverbs 3:11-12, 20:1; Mark 11:25-26; John 3:18; Romans 8:1, 5-7, 12:19; 2 Corinthians 5:7; Ephesians 4:26, 5:18; Hebrews 12:5-8; James 1:22, 26

Revelations of God's Love

Love's Questionnaire

Answer the following questions by placing a check under yes or no.

	Yes	No
Are you saved?		
Have you ever lied?		
Have you stolen anything?		
King David had a baby by the wife of one of his loyal soldiers, and then had him killed. Should he be forgiven?		
Tamar had a child by her father-in-law. Could she be in the genealogy of Christ?		
Lot's daughters got him drunk and had children by him. Should they be forgiven?		
Rahab, the harlot, and her household were saved when Israel invaded Jericho. Should she have been spared?		
Judas betrayed Jesus. Did he have a chance to repent?		
Do you harbor, carry, or retain jealousy?		
Do you judge people and situations before knowing all the facts?		

All we like sheep have gone astray; We have turned, every one, to his own way; And the Lord has laid on Him the iniquity of us all.
—Isaiah 53:6

For all have sinned and fall short of the glory of God.
—Romans 3:23

Gail P. Miller

If you answered "yes" to any of these questions, God has a place at the cross and in His kingdom just for <u>you</u>!

Love's Health Plan

Bless the Lord, O my soul; and all that is within me, bless His holy name! Who satisfies your mouth with good things, so that your youth is renewed like the eagle's.
—Psalm 103:1,5

Keep your heart with all diligence, for out of it springs the <u>issues of life</u>.
—Proverbs 4:23

All the days of the afflicted are evil, but he who is of a merry heart has a continual feast.
—Proverbs 15:15

Pleasant words are like a honeycomb, Sweetness to the soul and health to the bones.
—Proverbs 16:24

A <u>merry heart</u> does good, like medicine, but a broken spirit dries the bones.
—Proverbs 17:22

You will keep him in perfect peace, whose mind is stayed on You because he trusts in You.
—Isaiah 26:3

Therefore do not worry, saying "What shall we eat? or What shall we drink? or What shall we wear?" For after all these things the Gentiles seek. For your heavenly Father know that you have need all these things. But <u>seek first the kingdom of God</u> and His

righteousness, and all these things shall be added to you. Therefore do not worry about tomorrow, for tomorrow will worry about its own things. Sufficient for the day is its own trouble.
—Matthew 6:31-34

A good man out of the good treasure of his heart brings forth good; and an evil man out of the evil treasure of his heart brings forth evil. For out of the abundance of the heart his mouth speaks.
—Luke 6:45

<u>*Be anxious for nothing*</u>*, but in everything by prayer and supplication, with thanksgiving, let your request be made known to God; and the peace of God, which surpasses all understanding, will guard your hearts and minds through Christ Jesus.*
—Philippians 4:6-7

Therefore lay aside all filthiness and overflow of wickedness, and receive with meekness the implanted word, which is able to save your souls. But be doers of the word, and not hears only, <u>deceiving yourselves</u>. For if anyone is a hearer of the word and not a doer, he is like a man observing his natural face in a mirror; for he observes himself, goes away, and immediately forgets what kind of man he was. But he who looks into the perfect law of liberty and continues in it, and is not a forgetful hearer but a doer of the work, this one will be blessed in what he does.
—James 1:21-25

Revelations of God's Love

Love's Word is <u>your</u> medicine.
Take it daily!

Gail P. Miller

Love Draws with Loving Kindness

Show Your marvelous <u>loving kindness</u> by Your right hand, O You who save those who trust in You From those who rise up against them.
—Psalm 17:7

For Your loving kindness is before my eyes, And I have walked in Your truth.
—Psalm 26:3

How precious is Your <u>loving kindness</u>, O God! Therefore the children of men put their trust under the shadow of Your wings.
—Psalm 36:7

The Lord will command His loving kindness in the daytime, and in the night His song shall be with me-A prayer to the God of my life.
—Psalm 42:8

Because Your <u>loving kindness</u> is better than life, my lips shall praise You.
—Psalm 63:3

Who redeems your life from destruction, Who crowns you with loving kindness and tender mercies.
—Psalm 103:4

The Lord has appeared of old to me, saying "Yes, I have loved you with an everlasting love; therefore with <u>loving kindness</u> I have drawn you."
—Jeremiah 31:3

I will betroth thee unto Me forever; yes, I will betroth you to Me In righteousness and justice, in loving kindness, and mercy. I will betroth you to Me in faithfulness, and you shall know the Lord.
—Hosea 2:19-20

<u>Love</u> *suffers long and is* <u>kind</u>*; love does not envy; love does not parade itself, is not* <u>puffed</u> *up;*
—1 Corinthians 13:4

But the fruit of the Spirit is <u>love</u>*, joy, peace, longsuffering,* <u>kindness</u>*, goodness, faithfulness, gentleness, self-control. Against such there is no law.*
—Galatians 5:22-23

Loving kindness is God's magnet!

Gail P. Miller

Love Teaches

Then God said, 'Let Us make man in Our <u>image</u>, according to Our <u>likeness</u>; let them have <u>dominion</u> over the fish of the sea over the birds of the air, and over the cattle, over all the earth and over every creeping thing that creeps on the earth.
—Genesis 1:26

And the Lord God commanded the man saying, "Of every tree of the garden you may freely eat; <u>but of the tree of knowledge of good and evil</u> <u>you</u> <u>shall not eat</u>, for in the day that <u>you</u> eat of it <u>you</u> shall surely <u>die</u>."
—Genesis 2:16-17

This book of the law shall not <u>depart from your mouth</u>, but you shall <u>meditate</u> in it day and night, that you may <u>observe to do according</u> to <u>all</u> that is written in it. For <u>then</u> you will make your <u>way prosperous</u>, and <u>then</u> you will have <u>good success</u>.
—Joshua 1:8

You shall <u>tread upon</u> the lion and the cobra, The young lion and the serpent you shall <u>trample underfoot</u>.
—Psalm 91:13

No weapon formed against you <u>shall prosper,</u> and <u>every tongue</u> which rises against you in judgment You shall condemn. This is the heritage of the servants of the Lord, and their <u>righteousness is from Me</u>, Says the Lord.
—Isaiah 54:17

"And these signs will follow those who believe; In <u>My name</u> they will <u>cast out demons</u>; they will <u>speak with new tongues</u>; they will <u>take up serpents</u>; and <u>if they drink</u> <u>anything deadly</u>, it will by no means hurt them; they will <u>lay hands on the sick</u>, and they will recover.
—Mark 16:17-18

Behold, <u>I give you the authority</u> to trample on serpents and scorpions, and over <u>all the power of the enemy</u>, and nothing shall by any means hurt you. Nevertheless, do not rejoice in this, that the spirits are subject to you, but rather rejoice because <u>your names are written in heaven</u>.
—Luke 10:19-20

For the <u>weapons</u> of our warfare are not carnal but <u>mighty in God</u> for pulling down <u>strongholds</u>, casting down arguments and every high thing that exalts itself against the knowledge of God, bringing <u>every thought into captivity</u> to the obedience of Christ, and being ready to punish all disobedience when your obedience is fulfilled.
—2 Corinthians 10:4-6

"Put on the <u>whole armor of God</u> that you may be able to stand against the wiles of the devil. For we do <u>not wrestle against flesh and blood</u>, but against principalities, against powers, against the rulers of the darkness of this age, against spiritual host of wickedness in the heavenly places."
—Ephesians 6:11-12

<u>*Confess your trespasses*</u> *to one another, and pray for one another, that you may be healed. The effective, fervent prayer of a righteous man avails much.*
—James 5:16

Did <u>you</u> get love's lessons?

Revelations of God's Love

Love Can Be Followed

<u>Follow</u> (190, Greek ak-ol-oo-theh'-o) (a road) to be in the same way, to accompany (as a disciple) follow, reach

<u>Follow</u> (1377, Greek dee-o'-ko) (to flee) to pursue, to persecute; ensue, follow (after), given to, (suffer) persecute (-ion), press toward[61]

> *Because You have been my help, therefore in the shadow of Your wings I will rejoice. My soul <u>follows close behind</u> You; Your right hand upholds me.*
> —Psalm 63:7-8

> *He who follows righteousness and mercy Finds life, righteousness and honor.*
> —Proverbs 21:21

> *Listen to me, you who <u>follow</u> after righteousness, you who seek the Lord: Look to the rock from which you were hewn.*
> —Isaiah 51:1a

> *Then He said to them, "<u>Follow Me</u>, and I will make you fishers of men."*
> —Matthew 4:19

---

[61] *The New Strong's Exhaustive Concordance of the Bible*, James Strong's LL.D., S.T.D. Nashville, TN, Thomas Nelson Publishers, 1990.

Then Jesus said to His disciples, "If anyone desires to <u>come after</u> Me, let him deny himself, and take up his cross, and follow Me."
—Matthew 16:24

My sheep hear My voice, and I know them, and they <u>follow</u> Me.
—John 10:27

If anyone serves Me, let him <u>follow</u> Me; and where I am, there My servant will be also. If anyone serves Me, him My Father will honor.
—John 12:26

<u>Pursue</u> peace with all people, and holiness, without which no one will see the Lord.
—Hebrews 12:14 NKJV[62]

Is it hard for <u>you</u> to follow love?

---

[62] *New Spirit Filled Life Bible,* Jack W. Hayford, Li. D., Paul G. Chappell, Ph.D., Kenneth C. Ulmer, Ph. D., D. Min., Roy Hayden, Ph. D., Jonathan David Huntzinger, Ph. D., Gary Matsdorf, M.A., Thomas Nelson Bible, 2002.

Revelations of God's Love

The Fragrance of Love

Let him kiss me with the kisses of his mouth—For your love is better than wine. Because of the <u>fragrance</u> of your good ointments, your name is ointment poured forth; therefore the virgins love you.
—Song of Solomon 1:2-3

Your lips, O my spouse, Drip as the honeycomb; Honey and milk are under your tongue; And the <u>fragrance</u> of your garments is like the fragrance of Lebanon.
—Song of Solomon 4:11

I will heal their backsliding, I will love them freely, For My anger has turned away from him. I will be like the dew to Israel; He shall grow like the lily, and lengthen his roots like Lebanon. His branches shall spread; His beauty shall be like an olive tree, And his <u>fragrance</u> like Lebanon.
—Hosea 14:4-6

Then Mary took a pound of very costly spikenard, anointed the feet of Jesus, and wiped His feet with her hair. And the house was filled with the <u>fragrance</u> of the oil.
—John 12:3

Now thanks be to God who always leads us in triumph in Christ, and through us diffuses the <u>fragrance</u> of His knowledge in every place.
—2 Corinthians 2:14

For we are to God the <u>fragrance of Christ</u> among those who are being saved and among those who are perishing. To the one we are the <u>aroma of death</u> leading to death, and to the other the <u>aroma of life</u> leading to life. And who is sufficient for these things?
—2 Corinthians 2:15-16

Therefore be imitators of God as dear children. And walk in love, as Christ also has loved us and given Himself for us, an offering and a sacrifice to God for a <u>sweet-smelling aroma</u>.
—Ephesians 5:1-2

Indeed I have all and abound. I am full, having received from Epaphroditus the things sent from you, a <u>sweet-smelling aroma</u>, an acceptable sacrifice, well pleasing to God.
—Philippians 4:18

Is the aroma of love coming from <u>you</u>?

Love is a Weapon

And I will put enmity between you and the woman, and between your seed and her Seed; He shall bruise your head, and you shall bruise His heel.
—Genesis 3:15

But God demonstrates His own love towards us, in that while we were still sinners, Christ died for us. Much more then, having now been justified by His blood, we shall be saved from wrath through Him.
—Romans 5:8-9

For He must reign till He has put all enemies under His feet. The last enemy that will be destroyed is death. But thanks be to God, who gives us the victory through our Lord Jesus Christ.
—1 Corinthians 15:25-26, 57

Now all things are of God, who has reconciled us to Himself through <u>Jesus Christ</u>, and has given us the ministry of reconciliation, that is, that <u>God was in Christ reconciling the world to Himself</u>, not imputing their trespasses to them, and has committed to us the word of reconciliation.
—2 Corinthians 5:18-19

For though we walk in the flesh, we do not war according to the flesh. For the weapons of our warfare are not carnal but mighty in God for pulling down strongholds, casting down arguments and every high thing that exalts itself against the knowledge of God, bring every though

into captivity to the obedience of Christ, and being ready to punish all disobedience when your obedience is fulfilled.
—2 Corinthians 10:3-6

And you, being dead in your trespasses and the uncircumcision of your flesh, He has made alive together with Him, having forgiven you all trespasses, having wiped out the handwriting of requirements that was against us, which was contrary to us. And He has taken it out of the way, having nailed it to the cross. Having disarmed principalities and powers, He made a public spectacle of them, triumphing over them in it.
—Colossians 2:13-15

For <u>the Word of God</u> is living and powerful and sharper than any two-edged sword, piercing even to the division of the soul and spirit, and of joints and marrow, and is a discerner of the thoughts and intents of the heart.
—Hebrews 4:12

Are <u>you</u> using love as a weapon?

Chords of Love

*The Lord your God in your midst, The Mighty One, will save;
He will rejoice over you with gladness, He will quiet you with
His love, He will rejoice over you with singing.*
—Zephaniah 3:17

Gail P. Miller

Revelations of God's Love

Do You Need a Hug?

Your shoes and socks,
that's Me!

Your sleepwear and underclothes,
that's Me!

Your dress and pants,
that's Me!

Your belt and tie,
that's Me!

Your shirt and blouse,
that's Me!

Your sweater and jacket,
that's Me!

Your coat and hat,
that's Me!

Your scarves and gloves,
that's Me!

Your comb and brush,
that's Me!

Your jewelry and make-up,
that's Me!

Your sofa and chair,
that's Me!

Your bed and pillows,
that's Me!

Your blanket and sheets,
that's Me!

Gail P. Miller

Your car and other transportation,
that's Me!

Your body and spirit,
that's Me!

Your food and water,
that's Me!

Your breath and life,
that's Me!

Did you get it?

Love is closer than <u>you</u> think!

<u>Scriptures</u>
Genesis 1:1, 2:23-24; John 1:1-3; Colossians 1:16-17; Ephesians 3:20-21; Hebrews 1:2-3

Revelations of God's Love

Love's Grace Is Sufficient!

In your storm,
My divine influence
is sufficient for you.

In your pain,
My favor
is sufficient for you.

In your circumstance,
My benefits
are sufficient for you.

In your hardship,
My gifts
are sufficient for you.

In your darkness,
My graciousness
is sufficient for you.

In your problems,
My presence
is sufficient for you.

In your isolation,
My joy
is sufficient for you.

In your despair,
My pleasure
is sufficient for you.[63]

---

[63] *The New Strong's Exhaustive Concordance of the Bible*, James Strong's LL.D., S.T.D. Nashville, TN, by Thomas Nelson Publishers, 1990.

Gail P. Miller

In your disappointment,
My grace will
ward off obstacles for you.

In your failures,
My grace will
be enough for you.

In your weakness,
My grace will
avail for you.

In your trouble,
My grace will
lift you.

In your grief,
My grace will
satisfy you.

In your sickness,
My grace will
carry you.[64]

In all your temptations, trials, and tests,
the grace and sufficiency that
rest upon you
is…Me!

Scriptures
Matthew 5:11; 2 Corinthians 12:9; James 1:2-4; 1 Peter 4:14

---

[64] *The New Strong's Exhaustive Concordance of the Bible*, James Strong's LL.D., S.T.D. Nashville, TN, by Thomas Nelson Publishers, 1990.

Revelations of God's Love

Love Wants to Know!

Are you a Saul or a David?

Are you a Mary or a Martha?

Are you the prodigal son or the jealous older brother?

Are you law abiding or lawless?

Are you legitimate or illegitimate?

Are you spiritually minded or carnally minded?

Are you a lover of God or are you a hater of your brother?

Are you filled with His Spirit or are you filled with yourself?

Are you speaking the truth in love or are you a sounding brass or clanging cymbal?

All Scripture is given by inspiration of God, and is profitable for doctrine, for reproof, for correction, for instruction in righteousness.
—2 Timothy 3:16-17

Which one are <u>you</u>? Ask Love.

<u>Scriptures</u>
1 Samuel 15:1-26; Psalm 27:4, 37:4; Matthew 7:21-23; Luke 10:38-42, 15:11-32; 1 Corinthians 13:1; Romans 8:5-6, 9; 2 Timothy 3:16; Hebrews 12:8

Gail P. Miller

Love Was There!

When there was no heaven, earth, or mankind,
Love was there!

When you were formed in your mother's womb,
Love was there!

When you were born,
Love was there!

When you got your first tooth,
Love was there!

When your hair started to grow,
Love was there!

When you took your first step,
Love was there!

When you rode your first bike,
Love was there!

When you went to elementary, middle, and high school,
Love was there!

When you first fell in love,
Love was there!

When your heart was broken,
Love was there!

When you went to college, got a job, joined the military, or did nothing,
Love was there!

When you got married, divorced, became a widow, or remained single,
Love was there!

Revelations of God's Love

When you birthed your child,
Love was there!

When you were homeless,
Love was there!

When you were successful,
Love was there!

When you failed miserably,
Love was there!

When you experienced troubles, pain, and sickness,
Love was there!

When you lost a loved one,
Love was there!

When you move through each stage of life,
Love was, is, and will be there!

When your life is over here on Earth,

I will be <u>there</u>!

<u>Scriptures</u>
Genesis 1:26, 2:7; Psalm 90:1-2; Isaiah 44:24; Jeremiah 1:5; Hebrews 13:5; Revelations 1:8, 18

Gail P. Miller

Love's Trade Off!

Your way for
His way.

Your thoughts for
His thoughts.

Your needs for
His needs.

Your desire for
His desires.

Your unforgiveness for
His liberty.

Your hatred for
His love.

Your anger for
His peace.

Your despair for
His hope.

Your sin for
His righteousness.

Your life for
His life.

All of yours for
all of His!

Love is a back-and-forth, give-and-take process!

<u>Scriptures</u>
Isaiah 55:6-9; Romans 11:33-36; Galatians 2:20

Revelations of God's Love

Let Love Answer!

When anger knocks on the door of your heart,
 let Love answer!

When hatred knocks on the door of your heart,
 let Love answer!

When jealousy knocks on the door of your heart,
 let Love answer!

When covetousness knocks on the door of your heart,
 let Love answer!

When greed knocks on the door of your heart,
 let Love answer!

When revenge knocks on the door of your heart,
 let Love answer!

When malice knocks on the door of your heart,
 let Love answer!

When bitterness knocks on the door of your heart,
 let Love answer!

When wrath knocks on the door of your heart,
 let Love answer!

When self-righteousness knocks on the door of your heart,
 let Love answer!

When pride knocks on the door of your heart,
 let Love answer!

When arrogance knocks on the door of your heart,
 let Love answer!

When gossip knocks on the door of your heart,
 let Love answer!

Gail P. Miller

When lies knock on the door of your heart,
    let Love answer!

When lust knocks on the door of your heart,
    let Love answer!

When fornication knocks on the door of your heart,
    let Love answer!

When adultery knocks on the door of your heart,
    let Love answer!

When sexual immorality knocks on the door of your heart,
    let Love answer!

When unforgiveness knocks on the door of your heart,
    let Love answer!

When disobedience knocks on the door of your heart,
    let Love answer!

When Satan knocks on the door of your heart,
    let Love answer!

In like manner, fill <u>your</u> heart with Love!

<u>Scriptures</u>
Proverbs 6:16-19, 8:13; Psalm 119:11; Romans 5:5, 12:19-21; Ephesians 4:31-32, 5:1-5; Colossians 3:5-10; 1 John 4:4-18

Revelations of God's Love

Love Already Died!

Before there was a sound that could be heard,
Love had already died!

Before there was heaven and Earth,
Love had already died!

Before there was day or night,
Love had already died!

Before there were seas, oceans, lakes, rivers, streams, or water,
Love had already died!

Before there was a blade of grass, herb, tree, or bush,
Love had already died!

Before there was seedtime and harvest,
Love had already died!

Before there was a day, a year, or any element of time,
Love had already died!

Before there were any living creatures,
Love had already died!

Before there was evening or morning,
Love had already died!

Before there was anything and everything,
Love had already died!

Love
already had
His appointment with death!

Scriptures
Ecclesiastes 3:14-15; John 1:1-4; Colossians 1:16-18; Revelations 5:12, 13:8

Revelations of God's Love

It's Love's Word!

It is love's Word
 that is seen
 in the heavens.

It is love's Word
 that is seen
 in the Earth.

It is love's Word
 that is seen
 in the sun.

It is love's Word
 that is seen
 in the moon.

It is love's Word
 that is seen
 in the stars.

It is love's Word
 that is seen
 in the waters.

It is love's Word
 that is seen
in the flowers, plants, and trees.

It is love's Word
 that is seen
in light and darkness.

It is love's Word
 that is seen
in every living thing in the waters.

Gail P. Miller

It is love's Word
that is seen
in the birds of the air, the cattle of the field,
and every creeping thing.

It is love's Word
that is seen
in the wind, rain, hail, and snow.

It is love's Word
that is seen
in every man, woman, boy, and girl.

You, and all creation, are
a direct result of love saying,

"Let there be, there was, and it was very good!"

Scriptures
Genesis 1:1-31, 2:4, 7-9, 18-19; John 1:1-4; Colossians 1:16-17

There's No Competition!

You don't have to dress a certain way for
God's love.
You have it.

You don't have to fix your hair different ways for
God's love.
You have it.

You don't have to look like the world says for
God's love.
You have it.

You don't have to have any money for
God's love.
You have it.

You don't have to have lots of things for
God's love.
You have it.

You don't have to have a particular job for
God's love.
You have it.

You don't have to be known by anyone for
God's love.
You have it.

You don't have to compete for
God's love.
You have it.

What you have been longing for,
God has already given.

Love already has you!

Scriptures
Jeremiah 31:3; John 3:16-17; Romans 5:8; 1 John 4:8

Revelations of God's Love

Love Saves!

For God so loved the world that He gave His only begotten Son, that whoever believes in Him should not perish but have everlasting life. For God did not send His Son into the world to condemn the world, but that the world through Him might be saved.
—John 3:16-17

That if you confess with your mouth the Lord Jesus and believe in your heart that God has raised Him from the dead, you will be saved. For with the heart one believes unto righteousness, and with the mouth confession is made unto salvation. For whoever calls on the name of the Lord shall be saved.
—Romans 10:9-10, 13

Fill in the blanks with your name and then read the verses again.

For God so loved _____ that He gave His only begotten Son, that (if) _____ believes in Him should not perish but have everlasting life. For God did not send His Son into the world to condemn _____, but that _____ through Him might be saved.

Gail P. Miller

That if _____ confesses with his/her mouth the Lord Jesus and believes in his/her heart that God has raised Him from the dead, _____ will be saved. For with the heart _____ believes unto righteousness, and with the mouth confession is made unto salvation. For (if) _____ calls on the name of the Lord, _____ shall be saved.

Love truly wants you!
Love truly came for you!
Love truly waits for you!
Love truly made a way for you!
Love truly has feelings for you!
Love truly died on the cross for you!

Truly, you were designed for love!

Dewdrops of Love

Give ear, O heavens, and I will speak; and hear, O earth, the words of my mouth. Let my teaching drop as the rain, My speech distill as the dew, As raindrops on the tender herb, And as showers on the grass. For I proclaim the name of the Lord: Ascribe greatness to our God.
– Deuteronomy 32:1-3

Gail P. Miller

Revelations of God's Love

Hard Times!

Help me, Lord, to obey Your Word
in these hard times.

Help me, Lord, to stay the course
in these hard times.

Help me, Lord, to run this race
in these hard times.

Help me, Lord!
Help me, Lord!
Help me, Lord, in these hard times.

Help me, Lord, to apply Your understanding
in these hard times.

Help me, Lord, to focus on Your way
in these hard times.

Help me, Lord, to keep my eyes on You
in these hard times.

Help me, Lord!
Help me, Lord!
Help me, Lord, in these hard times.

In these hard times, I want to run.
In these hard times, I want to give up.
In these hard times, I think I won't make it.
In these hard times, my flesh rises to take over.

Help me, Lord!
Help me, Lord!
Help me, Lord, in these hard times.

Remember, I said, "I will never leave you nor forsake you."
I AM help!

Scriptures
Psalm 3:1-4, 18:6; 2 Corinthians 4:8-10, 10:4-6; 2 Timothy 2:3-7, 4:5; Hebrews 13:5-6

Revelations of God's Love

You Were Still Planned!

It wasn't a one-night stand.
You were planned!

It wasn't a mistake.
You were planned!

It doesn't matter if you don't know your father or mother.
You were planned!

It doesn't matter if you were put up for adoption.
You were planned!

It doesn't matter if you were reared by other family members.
You were planned!

It doesn't matter if you were born in or out of wedlock.
You were planned!

It doesn't matter if they hate you.
You were planned!

Whether they like you or not,
Whether they care for you or not,
Whether they see you or not,
Whether they speak to you or not,
Whether they love you or not,
Whether they claim you or not,
Whether they send for you or not,
Whether they accept you or not,
Whether they planned you or not,

You were still…His plan!

Scriptures

Genesis 1:26-28; Job 33:4; Psalm 24:1, 100:3; Acts 17:24-26; Ephesians 1:3-6

Revelations of God's Love

Every Day!

Every day,
He wants
to see you!

Every day,
He wants
to talk to you!

Every day,
He wants
to hear from you!

Every day,
He wants
to touch you!

Every day,
He wants
to hold you!

Every day,
He wants
to carry you!

Every day,
He wants
to provide for you!

Every Day,
He wants
to feed you!

Every day,
He wants
to be with you!

Gail P. Miller

Every day,
He wants
to be near you!

Every day,
He wants
to sit with you!

Every day,
He wants
to teach you!

Why?

Because He is your day!

<u>Scriptures</u>
Genesis 1:3-5; Psalm 119:105; Proverbs 2:1-9; John 1:1-4; 2 Corinthians 4:6-7; 2 Peter 1:19

Revelations of God's Love

You Are Unique!

Unique: the only one of its kind; unlike anything else.

I, _____, am the only one of my kind.
I am unlike anyone or anything else.
I am distinctive.
I am an individual.
I am special.
I am a misfit.
I am the sole, single, and lone one.
I am unrepeatable.
I am solitary.
I am exclusive.
I am peculiar.
I am rare.
I am uncommon.
I am unusual.
I come once-in-a-lifetime.[65]

I am His creation!

Scriptures
Genesis 1:26; Psalm 139:14; Romans 11:29; 1 Corinthians 12:4-12; Ephesians 2:10

---

[65] *High School Dictionary*, Thorndike-Barnhart, Scott, Fifth Edition, Foreman and Company 1968.

Gail P. Miller

Take A Look!

Now, take a look at how I
fashioned your head, perfectly designed to communicate Christ's mind,
so the leadership of My Kingdom will be a sign.

Now, take a look at how I
shaped your face with all its details tailor made,
so the light from My Son would be your aide.

Now, take a look at how I
selected the color and texture of your hair and sowed each strand,
so the story of My glory is made by hand.

Now, take a look at how I
structured your nose with nasal passages, cavities, and airways,
so the inhale and exhale of My breath would last all your days.

Now, take a look at how I
drew your brows near the tops of your eyes,
so they capture My expressions of heaven's cries.

Now, take a look at how I
hollowed holes for your eyes in the front of your body,
so My handy work is seen by everybody.

Now, take a look at how I
covered your eyes with lids and arranged lashes on the top and bottom,
so My sweet sleep will not be a problem.

Now, take a look at how I
molded your ears with channels and necessary parts,

Revelations of God's Love

so you can hear My voice from your heart.

Now, take a look at how I
designed your mouth with not one, but two, sets of teeth,
so you can taste of My goodness I chose to bequeath.

Now, take a look at how I
composed the harmony of your voice,
so My praise would come from you by choice.

Now, take a look at how I
fastened your lips to cover your mouth,
so the prayers from My temple would go east, west, north, and south.

Now, take a look at how I
knitted your head, neck, and body to form your human suit,
so My likeness would produce after our kind of fruit.

Now, take a look at how I
crafted and carefully made your image,
so My plan for you is to be My special tillage.

Now, what do you see?
The resemblance of Me.

<u>Scriptures</u>
Genesis 1:26a, 31; Psalm 139:13-16; Proverbs 20:12; 2 Timothy 3:16-17

Gail P. Miller

Do You Have the I-Dust?

I have needs.
I want what I what.
I can't do that.
I must have it.
I want you to do it for me.
I am in charge.
I forgot.
I heard that already.
I know what I'm talking about.
I have what it takes.
I did that before.
I would if I could.
I should but I won't.
I am busy.
I don't have time.
I will do it later.
I don't want to.
I'm not doing that.
I have my own opinion.
I believe and think like this.
I have my own ways.
I have a fresh word.

I am a bishop, apostle, evangelist, pastor, or deacon. I am a professional athlete, doctor, principal, or supervisor. I own a company. I am rich. I am famous. I have it going on.

I and *I* and *I* and *I* and *I*.

Love knows that your *I* is made of dust.

<u>Scriptures</u>
Genesis 2:7, 3:19; Psalm 78:38-39, 103:14; Isaiah 55:8-9; Romans 12:3-4; 1 Corinthians 1:11-13, 15:47-49

Gail P. Miller

From the Beginning of Time!

It is I, God,
Who keeps the earth on its axis.

It is I, God,
Who causes the sun to shine giving you light.

It is I, God,
Who lights the night skies with the moon so you can rest.

It is I, God,
Who twinkles the stars to display My love for you.

It is I, God,
Who calls clouds, rain, and snow to cover the Earth to give shade, food, water, and rest.

It is I, God,
Who sounds thunder and projects lighting across the heavens to reveal My power.

It is I, God,
Who keeps oceans, seas, lakes, and rivers filled for you to drink, clean, wash, play, travel, and admire My beautiful view.

It is I, God,
Who communicates with trees, plants, and vegetables to bring forth My harvest.

It is I, God,
Who causes the womb to break forth with life whether mankind, fish, bird, beast, or creeping things.

It is I, God,
Who gives every man, woman, boy, and girl breath and a limited time to recognize Who I AM.

Therefore, pay attention to Who time is.

<u>Scriptures</u>
Genesis 1:1-31; John 1:1-3, 10:27; Colossians 1:16-17; Hebrews 1:2-3

Gail P. Miller

His Glory was Seen!

When God used the rainbow to
establish His covenant to not destroy the world by flood,
His Glory was seen!

When Moses went on Mount Horeb
to see the unconsumed burning bush,
His Glory was seen!

When the Lord went before the children of Israel
as a pillar of cloud by day and a pillar of fire by night,
His Glory was seen!

When the Lord came down to Mount Sinai with thunder,
lightning, a cloud of smoke, and quaking,
His Glory was seen!

When God's mighty hand
brought the children of Israel out of Egypt,
His Glory was seen!

When the cloud covered the tabernacle
and Moses was not able to enter it,
His Glory was seen!

When King Solomon, the chief fathers, the priests, and the
children of Israel
finished building God's house,
His Glory was seen!

When Solomon finished praying, fire came from heaven,
consumed the burnt offering and sacrifices,
His Glory was seen!

Revelations of God's Love

When the shepherds watched their flocks and heard by night the Angel of the Lord and a multitude of angels give the message of Christ's birth,
His Glory was seen!

When Jesus was on the cross and breathed His last breath, and said, "Father, into Your hands I commit My Spirit,"
His Glory was seen!

Jesus is God's Glory
and this same glory can be seen in — and on — you!

<u>Scriptures</u>
Genesis 9:8-17; Exodus 3:1-6, 13:21, 19:9-20, 32:11, 40:34-35; 1 Kings 8:1-13; 2 Chronicles 7:1; Luke 2:8-14, 23:44-47; Romans 8:11

Gail P. Miller

Have You Seen Yourself?

Have you seen yourself?
I hadn't.
I could only go by what I saw when I looked down on myself.

Have you seen yourself?
I hadn't.
I could only go by the version of myself I saw reflected in a mirror.

Have you seen yourself?
I hadn't.
I could only go by what people told me I looked like.

Have you seen yourself?
I hadn't.
I could only go by what I saw when I glanced into a window as I passed by it.

Have you seen yourself?
I hadn't.
I could only go by what society said based on the color of my skin, my financial status, and where I lived.

Have you seen yourself?
I hadn't.
I could only go by how a teacher labeled me when she had me placed with other "special" students.

Have you seen yourself?
I hadn't.
I could only go by the images I saw in books, magazines, or on TV.

Revelations of God's Love

Have you seen yourself?
I hadn't.
I could only go by what my parents, siblings, friends,
classmates, spouses, neighbors, co-workers, church folk,
social systems, and strangers said about me.

Have you seen yourself?
I hadn't.
Until I opened God's Word and
Peered into it to look for myself.
I dug deep into it to find myself.
I searched and studied it to reveal myself.
In His Word is where I saw glimmers of myself.
I saw a likeness of myself.
I saw an image of myself.
I saw a resemblance of myself.
I saw the shape of myself.
I saw the manner of myself.
I saw the model of myself.
I saw a replica of myself.
I saw a clear view of myself.
I saw a focused future for myself.

For the first time,
I saw myself.
I saw my comparison.
I saw my similitude.
I saw my figure.

I saw my beginning and my ending.
I saw to whom I belonged.
I saw of whom I came.

Gail P. Miller

I saw my identity rising to the surface.
I saw the One I was patterned after.
I saw the true reflection of myself...in Jesus.

Have I seen myself?
Finally, after all this time,
I realized that I had been looking at myself
in the wrong mirror!

<u>Scriptures</u>
Genesis 1:26-27, 2:21-25, 5:1-2; Deuteronomy 30:9-10; Psalm 23, 90:1-2, 139:13-16; Proverbs 1:7, 3:5-8, 4:5-9; Isaiah 49:15-16; Matthew 5:3-12, 18:12-14, 19:4-6; Luke 10:19-20; John 3:16-17, 15:5, 9-15; Acts 17:11; Romans 8:14-17; 2 Corinthians 3:17-18; Ephesians 1:3-12; Colossians 1:17-18; 2 Timothy 2:15; James 1:2-5; 1 John 4:4, 17, 19

Revelations of God's Love

No Other Name!

You can worship other gods,
but there is no Salvation in it!

You can serve other gods,
but there is no Salvation in it!

You can call on the names of other gods,
but there is no Salvation in it!

You can praise other gods,
but there is no Salvation in it!

You can study about other gods,
but there is no Salvation in it!

You can bend your knees to other gods,
but there is no Salvation in it!

You can pray to other gods,
but there is no Salvation in it!

You can dance before other gods,
but there is no Salvation in it!

You can have festivals for other gods,
but there is no Salvation in it!

There is only One Name
under heaven
whereby mankind can be saved.

Jesus!

<u>Scriptures</u>
Exodus 34:14; Isaiah 43:11, 57:15; Hosea 13:4; Acts 4:9-12; 1 Corinthians 15:55-56; 2 Corinthians 5:21; 1 Timothy 2:5; 2 Timothy 2:10, 3:15

Gail P. Miller

It's Not Just!

It's not just
dye, ink, and imprints.

It's not just
letters, numbers, and words.

It's not just
phrases, punctuation marks, and grammar.

It's not just
sentences, questions, and paragraphs.

It's not just
verses, chapters, pages, and books.

It's not just
similes, metaphors, imageries, and figures of speech.

It's not just
parables, allegories, and a literary work.

It's not just
Hebrew, Greek, and Aramaic.

It's not just
wisdom, knowledge, and understanding.

It's not just
laws, statues, testimonies, and commands.

It's not just
poetry, writings, prophecies, and the gospels.

It's not just
the Old Testament and the New Testament.

It's not just
about relationships, fellowships, and communion.

Revelations of God's Love

It's not just
about the past, present, and future.

It's not just
about God's love, passion, salvation, and intimacy.

It's not just
about people, places, and things.

"Then I said, 'Behold I have come. In the volume of the book, it is written of Me to do Your will, O God.'"
(Psalm 40:7-8a)

It's Me…
Jesus.

Scriptures
Genesis 1:1; John 1:1-3; 2 Corinthians 4:6-7; Ephesians 1:20-23; Colossians 1:16-17; Hebrews 1:1-3, 10:7; Revelation 1:8, 11, 18

Gail P. Miller

We Still Have!

This poem was given to me by the Holy Spirit to read at the home going service of one of my best friends and long-time prayer partner.

In loving memory of Valeria Turner
December 23, 1953 – December 26, 2021

We still have
the memories of her beautiful smile
and her infectious laugh.

We still have
the effects of her fervent, heartfelt,
powerful prayers.

We still have
the words of conversations
with her.

We still have
the wisdom, knowledge, and spiritual understandings
she taught.

We still have
the values and examples she set as a daughter, sister,
wife, mother, grandmother, friend, co-worker,
and sister in Christ!

We still have
glimpses of her in videos and pictures at vacations, social
events, church, home, and
general times together.

Revelations of God's Love

But most of all,
the memory of her life points directly to
salvation in Christ Jesus the One with Whom she lives.

Valeria's life is still telling us to give our lives totally over to Christ. Why?

Because we still have time!

Also, in loving memory of her grandson,
Christopher A. Gwynne.

Gail P. Miller

Acknowledgements

I thank the Lord for using me to share His love.

I express my gratitude to my pastor, Dr. Diane M. Parks-Love, Rev. Thelma Buchanan, Deacons Connie Beal, Shavon Norvell, and the saints at Liberated in Christ Ministries.

Many thanks to Mr. Cory Ferguson, the staff, and students at East Dayton Christian School for allowing me to minister to you over the years.

Thanks to Marcia Ehlers, Marcia Raglin, Michelle Collier, Tiffany Collie Bailey, Ashlyn Young, Juanita Dozier, Stephen Smith, Sarina Tacovic, Twana Moreland, Nancy Crocett, Pastor Steve & Amy Walker, Tara Savage, and the staff and volunteers at the Good Neighbor House.

I thank Major Stanley and Gayle Senak, William "Kip" More (in memoriam), Corinne Dupree, Dwayne Hansbro, Michael "Silk' E Milk" Jackson, Erin May, Seth Gilley, Mark Anderson, Dorian Hoover, Karen Syring, Ann Woodfork, Lydia Ward, Kenisha Hinesmon, Ron Rowland, Joe Hartenstein, Tony Anderson, Bob Geter, John Goodloe, my student, Lemicha Brown, and the staff at the Ray & Joan Salvation Army Kroc Center.

I express my appreciation to Pastor Ivan and Gloria Love at Ministry of Love, Elder Dr. Charles and Ruby Byrd at Apostolic House of Christ, Sister Junica Jackson-Woods (at Grace Outreach Fellowship Church), Pastor Charles Foster, Brother Donald McKinney at Mt. Calvary Missionary Baptist Church and Graciela McLaughlin at Amazing Grace Empowerment Ministries.

Gail P. Miller

To my precious friends, Quinton, LaVette, Caleb, and Kenaz Smith, Thurman, Charlene and Nathan Leggs, JL and Vernell Dubose, Brenda Bentley, Marry Cleveland, Frances Winborn, Peter and Shawn Pullen, Romaine Sturgies, Norris and Diane Cole, Norris Cole Jr., Loretta Richardson, and Samuel H. Clayborne, thank you for your endearing friendship.

In loving memory of Russell McNeil, Mrs. Elizabeth C. Hall, James A. Hall, Joshua S. Aytch, Lillian Armour, Rev. Sennie B. Taylor, Robert H. Taylor II, Deborah K. Taylor, Ann R. Taylor, Myron K. Taylor, Sr., Myron K. Taylor, Jr., Vernon Richardson, Eric Love, Mother Carolyn Wheat-Moore, Mona A. Phillips, Peggy L. Phillips, and Mrs. Josie B. Battle. You are greatly missed.

Special thanks to Valerie J. Lewis Coleman for your talent, gifting, and expertise in publishing bestsellers and making what God has done through me, available to the world in book form.

About the Author

Gail P. Miller retired from Dayton Public and Jefferson Township Schools after thirty-seven years of service as a teacher. She has an associate degree in ministry from Liberated in Christ School of Ministry and a bachelor's degree in physical education from Central State University.

She volunteers with Child Evangelism Fellowship, The Good Neighbor House, Amazing Grace Empowerment Ministries, Ministry of Love, and the Salvation Army's Kroc Center.

She attends Liberated In Christ Ministries, Inc. under the leadership of Dr. Diane M. Parks-Love. Ms. Miller is a deacon, does evangelistic work, and operates in the gifts of giving and helps. She is a prayer warrior, spiritual midwife, and has answered the call to be a prophet of God.

Ms. Miller has one son, two grandsons, one great grandson, and one bonus granddaughter. She resides in Dayton, Ohio.

Ms. Miller's authored *True Love Has A Passion For You!* This series includes a book, journal, and study guide.

For copies of Ms. Miller's books or to request her to speak at your event, contact her at miller-gail@sbcglobal.net or PO Box 3751, Dayton, Ohio 45401-3751.

Gail P. Miller

About Queen V Publishing

The Doorway to YOUR Destiny!

Go thou and publish abroad the kingdom of God.
— Luke 9:60 ESV

Committed to transforming manuscripts into polished works of art, **Queen V Publishing** is a company of standard and integrity. We offer an alternative that allows the message in YOU to do what it was sent to do for OTHERS.

QueenVPublishing.com

Serving professional speakers and experts to magnify and monetize their message by publishing quality books

www.ingramcontent.com/pod-product-compliance
Lightning Source LLC
Chambersburg PA
CBHW071920290426
44110CB00013B/1420